BIBLE STUDY COMMENTARY

Leviticus-Deuteronomy

Bible Study Commentary

Leviticus–
Deuteronomy

M.GOLDSMITH

ARK PUBLISHING
130 City Road, London EC1V 2NJ

CHRISTIAN LITERATURE CRUSADE
Fort Washington, Pennsylvania 19034

©1981 **Ark Publishing** (UK dist.)
130 City Road, London EC1V 2NJ

Christian Literature Crusade (USA dist.)
Box C, Ft. Washington, PA 19034

First published 1981

ISBN 0 86201 085 3 (UK)
ISBN 0 87508 151 7 (USA)

Maps: Jenny Grayston

Phototypeset in Great Britain by
Filmtype Services Limited, Scarborough
Printed in U.S.A.

General Introduction

The worldwide church in the last quarter of the twentieth century faces a number of challenges. In some places the church is growing rapidly and the pressing need is for an adequately trained leadership. Some Christians face persecution and need support and encouragement while others struggle with the inroads of apathy and secularism. We must come to terms, too, with the challenges presented by Marxism, Humanism, a belief that 'science' can conquer all the ills of mankind, and a whole range of Eastern religions and modern sects. If we are to make anything of this confused and confusing world it demands a faith which is solidly biblical.

Individual Christians, too, in their personal lives face a whole range of different needs – emotional, physical, psychological, mental. As we think more and more about our relationships with one another in the body of Christ and as we explore our various ministries in that body, as we discover new dimensions in worship and as we work at what it means to embody Christ in a fallen world we need a solid base. And that base can only come through a relationship with Jesus Christ which is firmly founded on biblical truth.

The Bible, however, is not a magical book. It is not enough to say, 'I believe', and quote a few texts selected at random. We must be prepared to work with the text until our whole outlook is moulded by it. We must be ready to question our existing position and ask the true meaning of the word for us in our situation. All this demands careful study not only of the text but also of its background and of our culture. Above all it demands prayerful and expectant looking to the Spirit of God to bring the word home creatively to our own hearts and lives.

This new series of books has been commissioned in response to the repeated requests for something new to follow on from Bible Characters and Doctrines. It is now over ten years since the first series of Bible Study Books were produced and it is hoped they will reflect the changes of the last ten years and bring the Bible text to life for a new generation of readers. The series has three aims:

1. To encourage regular, systematic personal Bible reading. Each volume is divided into sections ideally suited to daily use, and will normally provide material for three months (the exceptions being Psalms and 1 Corinthians-Galatians, four months, and Mark and Ezra-Job, two months). Used in this way the books will cover the entire Bible in five years. The comments aim to give background information and enlarge on the meaning of the text, with special reference to the contemporary relevance. Detailed questions of application are, however, often left to the reader. The questions for further study are designed to aid in this respect.

5

2. To provide a resource manual for group study. These books do not provide a detailed plan for week by week study. Nor do they present a group leader with a complete set of ready-made questions or activity ideas. They do, however, provide the basic biblical material and, in the questions for further discussion, they give starting points for group discussion.

3. To build into a complete Bible commentary. There is, of course, no shortage of commentaries. Here, however, we have a difference. Rather than look at the text verse by verse the writers examine larger blocks of text, preserving the natural flow of the original thought and observing natural breaks.

Writers have based their comments on the RSV and some have also used the New International Version in some detail. The books can, however, be used with any version.

Introduction

Jews have always looked on the Pentateuch, the Torah, as the basis of their religious, social and personal life. It provides the background to our understanding of much in the development of biblical truth: sacrifice, the Law, the sabbath year, the year of Jubilee, etc. The key to this understanding, however, lies not only in the legal details, but in the basic principles set out in the Torah of man's covenant relationship with a holy God and of the need to live in holiness. The meticulous detail reveals the seriousness of these fundamental issues.

Leviticus, Numbers and Deuteronomy must be read in the context of the previous two books of the Pentateuch and the following historical books. The awe-inspiring revelation of God's glory and holiness at Sinai forms the prelude to the detailed laws of the sacrificial system and of daily living given in Leviticus and Numbers 1–10. Covenant relationship with a God of such burning holiness requires absolute care, even in the minute details of ritual – we dare not treat him with easy-going familiarity.

Numbers continues with the chronicle of Israel's wanderings through the wilderness, a weak and rebellious people whose temptations became a warning to the New Testament churches and so also to us (e.g. 1 Cor. 10:1-13 and Heb. 3). Inserted into the story of Israel's wanderings are more laws for God's people. Traditionally these laws have been divided into two categories, ritual and moral. But Israel was a theocracy – God was its Head of State – and in a theocracy such a clear-cut division can prove difficult. The New Testament writers had to battle out the Christian attitude to the Law. Clearly there is no salvation through the keeping of the Law but how far are we to obey the Old Testament laws?

Deuteronomy crowns the ministry of Moses with his final speeches to Israel which appear to be in the form of an old suzerainty treaty, that is, a treaty between a Great King and his vassals. These treaties were common up to the time of Moses in the neighbouring Hittite empire. Derek Kidner summarises their contents as: 'Preamble, historical survey, basic principles, detailed stipulations, confirmatory blessings and cursings, witnesses, and the injunction that copies of the covenant must be preserved and periodically read in public.' Preceded by oracles on the destiny of the twelve tribes, the closing chapters find their climax in the death of Moses himself. Thus the stage is set for Joshua. Israel is poised and ready for entry into and life in the promised land.

Analysis of Leviticus

1 The burnt offering

The tent of meeting. The background is in Exod. 40:34-38, where 'Glory' signified the presence of God in splendour in the midst of his people. We are faced immediately with an apparent contradiction – God in holy otherness and yet meeting with his people. Covenant relationship with Yahweh entails a balancing act. On the one side lies the abyss of exclusive emphasis on the terrifying holiness of God which cannot permit direct contact with sinful man. On the other side the quicksands of undue familiarity tempt unwary men to reduce God's glory to the shallow levels of human imagination. The tent of meeting, however, retained God's glory, both in his absolute holiness and in his gracious presence with man.

God met both with Israel as a total people and also with each individual Israelite. He desired to 'speak to the people of Israel' (2) and at the same time made provision for 'any man of you' to meet with him through the offering of sacrifice. Traditionally, western Christianity has overplayed the truth of God's dealings with individuals, neglecting the parallel truth of his interest in whole peoples. Some in Africa and Asia today swing the pendulum too far the other way. God *is* concerned for peoples, but he also meets with each one of us personally. He allows diminutive offerings of mere pigeons or turtledoves, so that no one is excluded by poverty from the presence of God. God loves the poor man's offering as much as the rich man's bull. What counts is the heart (Mark 12:41-44).

Sacrifice. For sinful man to meet with God requires sacrifice. Atonement is needed: sin must be covered. God is too holy to contemplate sin (Hab. 1:13). The burnt offering means literally 'that which ascends'. Through the sacrifice there rises a 'pleasing odour to the Lord' (9,13,17).

Some critics would parallel the levitical ordinance of the burnt offering with the Gilgamesh epic in the Babylonian flood legend where the gods hover like flies round the fragrant offering. But Leviticus avoids such crudity, although it, too, shows God being appeased and pleased by the fragrance of the burnt offering.

The burnt offering assumed man's intimate participation in the horror of sacrifice. The offerer laid his hands firmly on the head of the doomed animal and himself applied the knife. He could not remain coolly detached from the consequences of sin.

It should also be noted that the burnt offering was wholly for God. In contrast to the cereal and peace offerings (chapters 2 and 3), man might not eat any part of it.

2 The cereal offering

The term 'cereal offering' is a translator's convenience, for the Hebrew term simply means a present or an offering (e.g. Gen. 32:13; 43:11 and 2 Sam. 8:2). Although sometimes used of mere human gifts, it generally refers to offerings to God. In the levitical law it was only used of those offerings in which blood was not shed and which did not therefore signify atonement. In Genesis 4:4,5, however, the word is applied to the offerings of both Cain and Abel.

Wild, uncultivated produce could not be used in the cereal offering. We dare not give to God that which costs us nothing – a lesson David had evidently learned (2 Sam. 24:24). David said this in connection with the burnt offering, but it was more specifically so with the cereal offering. The Israelites were to offer what had been made by them from ingredients which they had grown. 'Man-made' was an essential qualification. S. H. Kellogg in his commentary on Leviticus comments that 'all the results and products of our labours, even in secular things' are thus offered to God. Israel knew no false division between secular and spiritual. Our daily tasks are God's call to us and are to be laid on the altar before him.

As is also the case in Numbers 15:1-10 and Leviticus 6:14-23 the cereal offering comes after the blood sacrifice of the burnt or sin offering. We can only dedicate our daily work to God when we have been made clean through the shedding of blood. Atonement precedes consecration.

If man is to approach God, a mediator is needed. Here we see the role of the levitical priesthood in presenting the people's sacrifices. Happily today, since the priestly work of Christ is complete, we need no other mediator. There is no need for mediating sacrificial priests in the Christian church. In the Old Testament, however, priests were still required and they were allowed to gain their food from the sacrifices (10).

The cereal offering consisted of corn and oil – even poor people would have these fundamental ingredients. But there was to be no leaven or honey. Leaven has the idea of sin, while honey, too, leads to fermentation and decay of the whole lump (as Kellogg points out). Over the whole offering there was frankincense, an ingredient of incense. This suggests prayer (Ps. 141:2; Luke 1:10; Rev. 5:8).

THOUGHT: As we go to our work, let us present our cereal offering with incense, but with no leaven.

3 The peace offering

Atonement in the burnt offering led on to the consecration of daily life and work in the cereal offering. Then came the festive peace offering when men could feast together in the joyful peace which resulted from the previous two offerings. Only on the basis of the burnt offering could there be peace. The fat of the peace offering was therefore burnt 'on the altar upon the burnt offering' (5).

The Septuagint translation of 3:5 is a direct parallel with Ephesians 5:2. On the basis of the fragrance of Jesus' sacrifice we can know the peace of walking in love. Because of the resurrection, we know that the crucified Christ was 'a pleasing odour to the Lord'. He 'was put to death for our trespasses and raised for our justification. Therefore . . . we have peace with God' (Rom. 4:25; 5:1). Peace is one of the great characteristics of God and therefore of the Christian gospel (e.g. Rom. 10:15; 15:33).

Kellogg points out that the peace offering was to terminate in 'a festive sacrificial meal, to express the conception of friendship, peace and fellowship with God'. In an Asian culture eating together signifies fellowship. Our fellowship with God leads to a loving unity with our fellow believers. This can be so enriching that it becomes an aim in our proclamation of Christ (1 John 1:3).

Peace and fellowship still rest on holy purity. The sacrifice must be 'without blemish' (1,6). The blood, with all its atoning significance of life and death, remained wholly for God. No explanation is given as to why the fat was also for him alone. Was the fat considered the tastiest portion (as in Chinese culture)? Andrew Bonar seeks to demonstrate this in his commentary. Compare also Genesis 4:4 and 1 Samuel 15:22. To God belongs the best of our time, talents and possessions – then we may enjoy his peace in fellowship together.

CHALLENGE: To God belongs the best of our time, talents and possessions.

4 The sin offering

The sin offering removed the guilt of unwitting sins. May it therefore be assumed that the burnt offering was for deliberate sins? Job, however, offered burnt offerings against the possibility of some undetected sins in his family (Job 1:5). In his careful concern not to transgress God's laws, the Jew was not only to hedge the Law around with a multitude of detailed commentary, but also to fear unconscious sins. So David prayed in Psalm 19:12 both with regard to undiscerned, hidden faults and also to presumptuous sins. Pharisaism could only see judgement for definite and purposed sin. What a contrast between the rabbinic 'there is joy before God when those who provoke him perish from the world' (Siphré, ed. Friedmann P-37) and the word of Christ (Luke 15:7,10). In the context of the sin offering Numbers 15:22-31 also draws the distinction between unwitting sin, for which the sin offering suffices, and high-handed, God-despising sin, for which a man must be cut off from Israel.

Only when the unwitting sin was discovered and made known was the sin offering to be brought (14,23,28). Anguished introspection was thus avoided. *God* may search and try us to see whether there be some hidden wickedness in us (Ps. 139:23), but *we* are not to indulge in such a search ourselves. The Holy Spirit will uncover to us our sins in due time – then we can rest in the sure efficacy of Christ, the perfect offering for sin. Through the shedding of blood comes atonement; atonement brings forgiveness (20,26,31,35).

A bull or a goat? The high priest, as the anointed leader of the covenant people, brought a bull for his sin offering. Likewise a bull was required for the sin offering of the whole congregation of God's people. Sin by a ruler or by one of the common people found forgiveness through a mere goat. Sin in the life of the church or by a leader of God's people is of grave concern to God.

THOUGHT: Hebrews 13:11-13 draws telling lessons from the words 'outside the camp' (12,21). 'Follow me,' Christ said.

5:1–6:7 Sin offering and guilt offering

At first sight there is a clear division in this passage. 5:1-13 appears to continue the previous chapter's legislation for the sin offering, while 5:14–6:7 proceeds to the guilt offering. However 5:6,7 relate to the guilt offering, although the total context of these verses is the sin offering. Likewise, the sins to which the guilt offering is related seem closely akin to those of the sin offering. Some commentators have suggested that the sin offering was for sins against God, while the guilt offering dealt with those against one's neighbour. Although this is fundamentally true, 6:1-7 shows that deceiving one's neighbour is in fact 'a breach of faith against the Lord' (6:2) and therefore the guilt offering must be brought 'to the Lord' and 'the priest shall make atonement for him before the Lord' (6:7). 'Unwittingly' remains a key concept in both sacrifices. The close relationship between these two distinct sacrifices is reflected later in the Mishnah where the two are frequently mentioned together.

The Hebrew for the guilt offering (*Asam*) implies the payment of compensation. Deceiving or robbing one's neighbour could not be rectified merely by sacrifice to the Lord, but must also include restoration plus the addition of a further fifth (6:5). See Matthew 5:23-26 for a New Testament application of this principle.

Andrew Bonar points out that the guilt offering was always a ram. He suggests that 'it was thus fitted to remind Israel of Abraham's offering of Isaac, when the ram was substituted'. He further notes that the blood was always put on the sides of the altar, not on the horns as in the sin offering. Bonar attributes this to the less public nature of those sins for which the guilt offering brought atonement.

TO THINK OVER: In this passage what sins are listed with regard to the sin offering and to the guilt offering?

OFFERING	PRINCIPAL REFERENCES	NATURE OF OFFERING
Burnt offering 'olah kalil	Leviticus 1;6:8-13	*Personal* Range of animals – bull for high priest to dove or pigeon. Animals were to be male and perfect. *Community worship* Two lambs daily, supplemented on the Sabbath and special feast days.
Cereal offering *minhah*	Leviticus 2;6:14-23 Numbers 15:1-12	Flour, baked cakes or roasted grain. Oil, incense and salt were also present but yeast and honey were specifically excluded.
Peace offering *zebah, shelamim* Three sub-divisions: thank offering, freewill offering, vow offering	Leviticus 3;7:11-18	Animal, male or female.
Sin offering *hattath*	Leviticus 4:1–5:13; 6:24-30	Range of perfect animals – from bull for high priest or whole community to lamb for private individual. For the poor, pigeons, doves or cereal offering.
Guilt offering *'asham*	Leviticus 5:14-19; 7:1-10	Perfect ram of appropriate value. Only for private individuals.

MAIN FEATURES	MEANING/ SIGNIFICANCE
The offerer provided own animal which must be perfect. The offerer killed his own animal and the blood was sprinkled on the altar by the priest. The whole offering was burnt on the altar. At some periods at least the burnt offering was to be accompanied by cereal offering and drink offering.	**Atonement** averting the wrath of God is the main idea. The offering also reflects the commitment of the worshipper – an element of costliness was involved.
Materials presented by the worshipper. A token part was burnt on the altar and the rest eaten by the priests. Sometimes the cereal offering was made alone and sometimes as an accompaniment to other sacrifices.	This is a **thanksgiving,** offering the basic commodities of life. The root meaning is related to the term gift. The cereal offering could, however, serve as a sin offering for the poor and the idea of atonement is never entirely absent.
Presented and killed by the worshipper. The blood was sprinkled on the altar by the priest, specified portions burnt on the altar and the remainder eaten by the priest and the worshipper. In the thank offering, a normal cereal offering and a cereal offering of cakes baked with yeast were included.	Might be a thank offering a freewill offering or an offering in fulfilment of a vow. In any case it speaks of **communion.** It is an expression of peace or wholeness, either enjoyed or desired.
Presented and killed by the worshipper. The blood sprinkled on the altar and specified portions burnt. The remainder eaten by the priest in the case of a sacrifice for the priest or community when it was burnt outside the camp.	**Purification** – cleansing from unintentional sin or sins of omission on the part of the individual or community.
As for sin offering.	**Reparation** – similar to the sin offering, but with the requirement to make restitution to an injured party.

6:8–7:10 Further regulations for the offerings

Today's and tomorrow's passages give further instructions to the priests on how the five offerings were to be conducted. We may feel that quite adequate detail was given in the previous chapters, but with such strong emphasis on holiness there must be no room for possible errors in the administration of God's holy offerings. Absolute and meticulous attention to detail was required lest God's holiness be contaminated. The priest was therefore to change his garments (10,11) and care was also to be taken over who touched any part of the offering (18) – holiness as well as sin is contagious. Even the joyful eating of the priests' portion had to be in a 'holy place' (7:6).

The offerings belonged utterly to God, but he then allowed certain portions to become the livelihood of the priests. God delights to lavish good things on his servants. Luxurious living does not befit the servant of God, but his honour is not furthered by unhappy poverty. As good stewards let us note the expression 'their portion of my offerings' (6:17).

When the priests acted as mediators in the cereal offering they were granted a share, but when they themselves offered the sacrifice it had to be wholly burned (6:18,23). We can never take back for our own use what we have given to God.

Note the refrain 'the Lord said to Moses' (6:1,8,19,24). The sacrificial system may well have been influenced by related systems in neighbouring nations, but Israel's sacrifices were expressly commanded by God and every detail was by his command. Both in Old Testament and New Testament there are examples of religious and cultural take-over bids. The danger is always syncretism, but careful teaching should ensure a right, God-centred theology. If the church is to relate effectively to its cultural and philosophical surroundings, it must learn to use the world's forms, taking care that Christ remains central and God's word is faithfully kept. Otherwise the church becomes an irrelevant cultural island.

QUESTION: How can we today combine friendly and joyful informality with a reverent awareness of the holy?

7:11-38 Further instructions for the peace offering

Chapter 3 concentrated on the peace offering as a pleasing odour acceptable to the Lord. This passage now mentions the ensuing meal and the priests' allotted portion. If our thinking on any subject is to be biblical it must be primarily God-centred.

Three motives underlay the peace offering. It could be a thanksgiving, a votive or a freewill offering. Resting on the already assured foundation of atonement the edifice of praise and thanksgiving could be erected. The feast after the thanksgiving peace offering was eaten on the same day (15). Kidner suggests that this ensured 'that the feast was shared, and shared widely'. After the votive and freewill offerings the meal could be kept for two days; this perhaps allowed a more intimate gathering.

As the Mishnah points out, the votive and freewill offerings are very similar (Megillah 1.6). The votive offering consists of that which has been given to God by vow; the freewill offering is voluntary. The Mishnah further legislates that if a freewill offering is lost or damaged before it is offered, it need not be replaced; but fourfold or fivefold restitution is demanded for a votive offering (Baba Kamma 7.4). Vows to God can be redeemed, but cannot be taken lightly.

The heave offering (14) and wave offering (30) were not special sacrifices, but rather particular methods of presenting the peace offering. Both signified a raising of the offering high before God. Bonar says the wave offering was waved in each direction to symbolise God's rule over the whole earth, but Kidner would seem more correct in suggesting that it was waved towards the altar and back with the symbolism of being offered to and then received back from the Lord.

What touched the unclean became itself unclean (19). What touched the holy became itself holy (6:27). Both principles have abiding truth (e.g. 1 Cor. 7:14).

CHALLENGE: Paul sees a continuity between the levitical sacrifices and Christian giving. Philippians 4:18 calls the church's gifts, 'a fragrant offering, a sacrifice acceptable and pleasing to God' – our giving delights God as well as supplying the church's needs. 2 Corinthians 9 talks of the 'cheerful giver' and a 'willing gift', reminding us of the freewill offering.

Questions for further study and discussion on Leviticus 1–7

1. List the sacrifices in these chapters and their basic significance.

2. List the component parts of each sacrifice (e.g. blood, fat, leaven, etc.) and their significance.

3. What New Testament parallels can you find to each of the sacrifices? How do they relate to us today?

4. 'We dare not offer to God that which costs us nothing' (see note on Lev. 2). Why do you think this is so? How did David learn this lesson (2 Sam. 24:24)? Are there areas in which we are in danger of doing that?

5. 'Our daily tasks are God's call to us' (see note on Lev. 2). In what ways should what we do and how we do it be affected by this fact?

6. Discuss the difference between anguished introspection and Christian repentance (see note on Leviticus 4).

7. In what ways today do Christians follow Christ 'outside the camp' (Hebrews 13:11-13 and Leviticus 4)?

8. The church must learn to use the world's forms while keeping Christ and his word central (note on Lev. 6). Discuss what this means.

8 Consecration of priests

The summary of the five offerings in 7:37 surprisingly includes 'the consecration'. This introduces the consecration or ordination of priests in Leviticus 8. Moses' consecration of Aaron and his sons (1-9) plus all that is connected with the sacrificial system (10-13) was followed by a sin offering (14-17), a burnt offering (18-21) and an ordination offering (22-29). The ordination offering included a wave offering (27) and involved the cleansing and consecration of the whole person through the symbolic placing of blood on the extremities of the body (23). The chapter concludes with the completion of the rite of consecration.

Aaron was robed with all the priestly garments to represent the twelve tribes and bring them into the presence of God (5-9). This included the Urim and Thummim which were to enable Aaron to discern God's mind and will. The priest was therefore not only to engage in a sacrificial ministry, but also to mediate the mind of God to his people. In the New Testament we have in Christ the privilege of direct access to God without priestly mediation; likewise we can 'have the mind of Christ' (1 Cor. 2:16).

'Consecration' is equivalent to sanctification. The heart of God's teaching in Leviticus is the concept of holiness. Priests were set apart for God's service; this paralleled the consecration of animals, vessels, clothing and the altar itself.

God was the author of the priests' consecration (1); Moses was his instrument. The whole congregation of God's people was present at the ordination. Democratic choice played no part, but the people had played an essential role in witnessing God's call through his servant Moses. Is this a pattern for ordination today? Or should structures of church order and government evolve according to cultural development? Does the Bible give an unchanging blueprint concerning such issues? These are fundamental questions not only for the planting of the church in mission areas, but also for the church in Britain today as it seeks to relate to contemporary society.

Basic to the consecration of priests was the anointing with oil (10-13). It signified dedication to God and commissioning for service (1 Kings 19:15,16); oil parallels the Spirit given to equip God's servants for his ministry (Isa. 61:1 and 1 John 2:27). The ideal anointed servant of God is the Messiah. We see, too, in the 'holy crown' (9) a picture of the royal priesthood of the Messiah, the Lamb upon the throne (Rev. 22:3).

9 The consecration completed

Ordination was no light-hearted ritual. The detailed requirements of chapter 8 led to the command to wait for seven days in the tent of meeting (8:33,35). Then on the eighth day (1) the culmination of the consecration began. Again the need for cleansing and holiness was underlined by further sin and burnt offerings for Aaron and his sons (2). Sacrificial offerings for the whole people of Israel (3-5) introduced Moses' climactic promise that 'the glory of the Lord will appear to you' (6). However, the fulfilment of such a promise required a further sequence of sacrifices. First Aaron as high priest needed a sin offering and a burnt offering (8-14). Only 'then' (15) could Aaron present acceptable offerings for the people (15-21). 'Then' (22) came the priestly blessing and the climax of the fulfilment of God's promise – 'the glory of the Lord appeared to all the people' (23). The Book of Hebrews draws the contrast between Aaron's need of sacrifices and the perfect adequacy of Jesus who is the perfect high priest as well as the spotless sacrifice.

Notice the sequence of Aaron's actions. 'Aaron drew near to the altar' (8) and 'presented the people's offering' (15); this was the necessary precondition to 'Aaron lifted up his hands toward the people and blessed them' (22). At his ascension Jesus too lifted up his hands and blessed his followers (Luke 24:50). Deuteronomy 21:5 shows such bene- dictions to be part of the calling of the priesthood. 'Bless' can become a weak word with little specific meaning, but Deuteronomy 28:1-14 details its definite content for Israel.

What is the glory of the Lord? The revealed splendour and utter holiness of God present in the midst of his people. This is also the theme of Ezekiel where the glory of the Lord starts with Israel, is gradually driven away by sin and finally returns with the climax of 48:35. Like Israel, we too can see the glory of the Lord (John 1:14). Glory is not only beauty and grace, but also holy fire and burning purity (24). Israel responded to such a revelation with a ringing shout of joyful worship and praise. They expressed awe and adoration by falling on their faces. The same word, 'fall', is used in Amos 3:5 to describe a bird swooping suddenly down from the heavens. The people of Israel fell like stones to the ground before the revealed splendour of God.

'The Lord commanded' (6,7,10) prepares us for the next chapter.

10 Disobedience in the priesthood

Disobedience and counterfeit contrast with the glory of chapter 9: 'unholy fire . . such as he had not commanded them' (1). The glorious words of v. 3 therefore became words of judgement instead of being words of blessing and joy. We are reminded of the double use of the name 'Emmanuel'. In Matthew 1:23 it is a saving revelation in Jesus, but in Isaiah 7:14 it is a threat to the disobedient Ahaz. God's presence in glory always spells discomfiture to the rebellious, but salvation to the faithful.

The ministry of the priesthood had many facets. Sacrifice and discernment of God's will have already been noted. Now the teaching responsibility of priests is stressed (11). Israel was to be taught 'all the statutes' (11), not just the fundamentals – note the parallel with Matthew 28:20 and Paul's testimony to this effect in Acts 20:27. The church's task of mission both in Britain and overseas includes such teaching and training as 'may present every man mature in Christ' (Col. 1:28).

The basis of the priestly teaching ministry was the distinction 'between the holy and the common and between the unclean and the clean' (10). To demonstrate this Aaron and his two remaining sons were not permitted the relief of bewailing God's judgement of Nadab and Abihu. God's reaction to their death differed from the natural agony of human reactions – and the priests were God's anointed (7). Likewise they were not to drink alcohol when they went into the tent of meeting (9). They were not commanded to be total abstainers, but 'no priest shall drink wine when he enters the inner court' (Ezek. 44:21).

Some sacrifices culminated in burning (16), some in the priests eating their portion (16-20). Thus the priests played a vital role in the presentation of these sacrifices. They shared in bearing Israel's sin before God and so in the ministry of atonement. As mediators between God in his holiness and man in his sin their responsibility was onerous. Absolute, exact obedience to God's ordinances was therefore demanded of the priests (1-3, 16-20).

THOUGHT: The greater our responsibilities in God's service, the more urgently we are called to obedience in holiness.

11 Food laws

In this chapter, 10:10 is further expounded and applied. Israel was given these food laws to illustrate this basic teaching that there is a distinction between the holy and the common. This is based on God's holy separateness from his creation which is stressed in the first two books of the Pentateuch. God's holy otherness does not preclude his intense concern for and involvement in the world, but it excludes a pantheistic reduction of God's purity. This separation is further seen in the distinction between God's covenant people and the nations around, between the church and the world. Separation does not mean uninvolved exclusiveness, but the edges should not be blurred. We need to be careful not to draw unbiblical conclusions from these scriptural principles – for example, a wrong distinction between 'secular' and 'spiritual' spheres of service. And we cannot forget that God is sovereign over *all* his creation, not just over the 'holy'.

Why were some animals clean and others unclean? What determined which fitted into each category? Some have maintained that the unclean animals had a foreign cultic background. More likely is the thesis that health questions determined the prohibitions. Contemporary feelings with regard to the various categories of animals may also have played a part. But clearly the primary purpose remained the daily underlining and illustration of the biblical teaching of holiness.

Blood always had special significance. Carnivorous animals were therefore included amongst those which could not be eaten (13-19, 27). Likewise physical contact with the dead body of any animal made a man unclean.

The word 'insects' (20-23) probably meant any small creature which went in swarms. Those that crawled could be eaten if they had jointed legs and could therefore hop. We can only smile at the RSV translation 'have legs above their feet'! The Hebrew signifies 'bend over' and thus implies joints in the leg.

This chapter finds its climax and deepest significance in verses 44 and 45. All depended on the nature of Yahweh, the holy God of Israel. He was their Redeemer who had brought them out of slavery in Egypt. We see a sequence – redemption and salvation, a covenant relationship as God's people, and therefore the command to be holy, 'for I am holy'. Ultimately man's holiness is dependent on the character of God, not just upon the observance of regulations.

12 Defilement by childbirth

As implied in the previous chapter, blood defiled and made a woman ritually unclean. The shedding of blood in menstruation and childbirth was not morally impure, but all shedding of blood required ritual purification. Sadly, this has often been misunderstood, so that some Christians have felt that natural processes should be forsaken if we desire truly holy living. Biblical holiness is anchored to life in the world and can be attained in and through the normal processes of life (1 Tim. 2:15).

Read Luke 2:21-40 to see the fulfilment of this chapter in the life of Jesus' family. Note the poor home into which he was born (8, compare Luke 2:24). Circumcision on the eighth day (3) was not only the sign of God's covenant promises, but also marked the occasion of the giving of a name (Luke 1:59 and 2:21). In Hebrew culture the name had deep significance. It denoted personal character and without it one was hardly a person. The Kenyan theologian John Mbiti points out therefore that circumcision in the Old Testament and baptism in the New Testament mark entry into God's people and the gift of a new nature and character. Incorporation into the community is a vital ingredient for real existence.

Commentators vary in their explanations of why the period of uncleanness for a baby girl (5) was double that for a baby boy (4). Some link this with the curse of woman after the fall; others suggest that the normal was eighty days, but this was halved for the boy because of the blessing of circumcision. Whatever the reason, the fact is sure that Hebrew society rejoiced doubly in the birth of a son.

In this chapter the burnt offering with its concept of dedication precedes the sin offering and the consequent atonement. This is the reverse of the usual sequence (e.g. 8:14-18; 9:7; 14:19). This underlines the fact that childbirth did not make a woman morally unclean, but merely ritually in need of cleansing. It may also have added the dimension of dedication as the new life was offered to God.

THOUGHT: Biblical holiness is anchored to life in the world and can be attained in and through the normal processes of life.

13 Defilement by 'leprosy'

Those who have experienced the scourge of leprosy will sympathise with the careful regulations of this chapter for any skin disease which could possibly cause the ravages of leprosy. However it is clear from the details given here that the range of skin diseases under consideration is not what we now call leprosy.

Some commentators suggest that ritual uncleanness is stressed in this chapter rather than the question of health. Thus N. Snaith in the *New Century Bible* Commentary claims that uncleanness from these skin diseases was due to the emergence of blood through the open sores. However, the incidence of open wounds is not the only reason given for pronouncing a man unclean. If the disease appeared to go deeper than just the skin or if the hair in the diseased place turned white (3); if the disease spread (7) and was therefore presumably contagious, then a man was declared unclean. And even those verses which state that uncleanness was due to the presence of open wounds have no specific mention of blood. The word 'blood' does not appear at all in this chapter.

However, it remains true that 'leprosy' in the Bible does have a symbolic significance. Leprosy is a picture of sin. We note therefore that the leprosy sufferer was to remain outside the camp, to dwell alone (sin always isolates men) and to adopt the outward signs of mourning (45,46), for the consequence of sin is death (Rom. 6:23). Neither sin nor leprosy is deemed incurable. By God's grace salvation and healing remain a bright hope (46). Here we observe also the close biblical relationship between salvation and healing.

In the assurance that the Old Testament has been fulfilled in Christ we must not be tempted to dismiss these chapters as irrelevant to us today. The principles of God's teaching in the Law retain their validity through all ages (Matt. 5:17-20). We observe not only the principle of isolation for contagious sin and disease, but also the practice of thorough examination by publicly recognised officials (4-6). The radical treatment of the disease in garments and cloth ('burn' – 52,55,57) is a picture of God's radical judgement of sin which may contaminate his people (e.g. Lev. 10:1-3; Acts 5:1-10).

14 The cleansing of 'leprosy'

1. In a human sufferer (1-20). The Talmud and Jewish tradition link the details of the cleansing ritual to the supposed causes of the disease. The twittering birds parallel chattering slander, for which the Talmud says leprosy is the punishment. The height of the cedarwood tree is a picture of pride, another cause of leprosy. Such idle fancies, however, damage the plain sense of Scripture and such allegorical interpretations of the Bible make it impossible for the normal man to read and interpret the Word for himself.

We would do well nevertheless to meditate on the true symbolism of the use of hyssop and the sprinkling of the blood. Likewise the living, running water and the release of one of the birds give cause for thought. Note that this bird has been dipped in the shed blood before being sent out – is this a parallel of the scapegoat?

We note not only the succession of sacrificial offerings which were necessary for the ritual cleansing of the former patient, but also the absolute care with which he was examined before he could be allowed to return to fellowship with society. He was examined twice with a week's interval and he was also required to shave off all his hair (8,9), so no remnant of the disease could lurk unobserved beneath the hair. So today, anyone with a contagious disease should be thoroughly investigated by a recognised official before he may return to normal social life.

2. In a poor sufferer (21-32). Once again we note the merciful provision of lesser offerings for those who could not afford the normal specified sacrifices. God is never concerned with how much we offer to him, but rather with the obedient and loving attitude which makes us 'cheerful givers' (2 Cor. 9:7). But the 'log of oil' (10,12,21,24) remained unchanged (it was equivalent to about ⅞ pint), for it conveyed a sense of overflowing royal bounty and grace.

3. In a house (33-53). The previous chapter ends with the possibility of disease affecting garments; now it may be discovered in the very fabric of a house. Note the apparently offensive idea that it was *God* who might put disease into a house (34). Traditionally Jews have explained this by asserting that God caused such fungoid growth in order to make the Jews pull down their walls and discover the gold which the Amorites had hidden inside the walls. There is a more likely explanation! God is sovereign over all and even evil is ultimately under his controlling hand.

15 Defilement by a discharge

The outline of this chapter is symmetrical. Abnormal discharges in the man (1-15) are dealt with before normal discharge (16-18): in the woman it is the reverse; the normal (19-24) precedes the abnormal (25-30). The chapter climaxes in the fundamental purpose of these laws (31) and then comes a brief summary of the whole (32,33).

With the leprosy laws it was discharge from the body which caused uncleanness. In this chapter 'body' (2,3) is a euphemism, for the Hebrew *basar* (flesh) clearly refers to the genital organs. The Greek equivalent of the Hebrew word for the man or woman who suffers from a discharge is *gonorrhues* which indicates the sort of disease which lay behind the abnormal discharge. Thus ritual and moral uncleanness became closely interrelated.

Normal discharges made the sufferer temporarily unclean, but they did not require the offering of sacrifices to make atonement. Only the abnormal discharge needed atonement. The regulations concerning the diseased virtually meant total exclusion from normal society – not quite as radical as in the case of leprosy, but still quite extreme.

These regulations were, again, essentially for ritual purposes, to maintain the distinction between the holy and the common. But they were also clearly related to health requirements. Uncleanness primarily affected whatever the man or woman sat or lay upon, although spitting (8) and touching with unrinsed hands (11) also imparted impurity.

In the light of these regulations it is helpful to reread the Gospel story of the woman with an issue of blood (Luke 8:43-48) with its emphasis on the word 'touch'. The Law isolated such a woman, but Jesus healed. The weakness of the Law necessitates the healing ministry of the Saviour.

At Sinai Israel had begun to learn the utter holiness of God. At Perez-uzzah they experienced God's judgement when Uzzah touched the ark (2 Sam. 6:6,7), the central feature of the tabernacle where God dwelt. Now the climax of our chapter is the realisation that the laws of defilement were given to prevent Israel from defiling God's tabernacle (31). Contact with the presence of the holy God can only mean death for unclean man. This principle underlies all the Old Testament teaching on sacrifice and atonement with its fulfilment in Jesus Christ's redemptive and reconciling work on the cross.

TO THINK OVER: The law isolated . . . but Jesus healed. What implications does that have for our attitudes and church life today?

Questions for further study and discussion on Leviticus 8–15

1. Observe the details of the Aaronic priesthood and apply these to Christ's and the Christian's call to be a royal priesthood.

2. What did the 'glory of the Lord' mean to the Jews of Moses' day? What did it mean to John and the New Testament writers? What does it mean to us? (See note on Lev. 9.)

3. In what way is Jesus the perfect High Priest (notes on Lev. 9; Heb. 4:14-16; 5:1-10; 7)?

4. What does the New Testament teach about food laws? See Matthew 15:10-20; Acts 10:9-16; Romans 14:13-23; Colossians 2:16-23.

5. How serious a disease is leprosy in the world today? Find out about the work of the Leprosy Mission. What are their needs?

6. How does the summary of Leviticus 15:31 strengthen Paul's words in 2 Corinthians 6:14–7:1? What are some practical applications of this today?

7. To some God has given the gift of teaching (Lev.10). How does teaching differ from preaching and witnessing? What does the New Testament say about teaching? What are the particular problems faced by RE teachers in schools? Make this a prayer topic.

8. 'God is sovereign over all and even evil is ultimately under his controlling hand' (see note on Lev. 14, compare Rom. 8:28). Discuss examples of this from the Scriptures and your own experience.

16 The way into the holiest

Atonement has been a crucial concept throughout the previous sacrificial ordinances, but nevertheless the sin of Aaron's two sons led to death (1). In this context the great Day of Atonement was instituted so that all Israel's sin could be covered (compare Ps. 32:1; Rom. 4:7). Without the covering of Christ's righteousness over our sin it is impossible to enter the holy presence of the King (Matt. 22:11-13).

Even Aaron, the high priest, could not enter the 'holy place within the veil' (2) without careful observance of God's ordinances concerning his apparel and ritual washing (4) and without a sin offering for himself (6-14). This was only acceptable because of the incense of humble prayer (13). Even with all these preparations Aaron was 'not to come at all times into the holy place' (2) and God's glory would still be wrapped 'in the cloud'.

Having offered the sin offering for himself, Aaron then proceeded to make atonement for the whole people and for the holy place itself, the tent of meeting and the very altar on which the sacrifices were offered. Everybody and everything needs atonement before God can be present with his people.

Traditionally Azazel (26) has come to be associated with the Devil, but the word actually implies 'removal' or 'going away'. One goat was slain as a sin offering while the other was sent away into the wilderness, bearing the sins of Israel (20-22). These two pictures of the sin-bearer removing the iniquity of God's people cannot but impress.

Throughout this chapter our minds go to Hebrews and the fulfilment of the atonement ordinances in the supreme person of Jesus Christ. The contrast of 'once for all' (Heb. 9:12) with the repeated and inadequate Aaronic atonement is fundamental – and at the Reformation became a key argument with regard to justification and the Holy Communion. The incomparable perfection of Jesus' atoning work as our High Priest and as the Lamb of God far outshines even the splendour of the Day of Atonement. Although majoring on the absolute and unique supremacy of Christ as High Priest and as the perfect sacrifice, Hebrews still looks forward to the ultimate climax of full salvation at his second coming (Heb. 9:28).

FOR MEDITATION: Even now let us glorify the Lamb!

17 Precious blood

Sacrifice to the Lord alone (1-9). The usual Hebrew word for 'sacrifice' originally meant 'slaughter'. All killing of animals had sacrificial significance. They could not be killed merely for food, but had first to be offered to the Lord. This passage is not aimed against secularism, in which the sacrificial element itself was neglected, but rather it opposes idolatrous offerings which could easily follow if Yahweh were neglected when sacrifices were made. Archaeological research has shown how easily Israel fell into the trap of adopting the false deities and religious practices of her neighbours. Virtually every Israelite settlement which has been unearthed has yielded a number of figurines and other idolatrous images. The 'satyrs' (7) seem to have been 'the goat demons of the countryside' (Snaith). The cults of the Canaanite deities were associated with male and female sacred prostitutes, so the imagery of playing the harlot was distressingly apt. Yahweh desired a perfect relationship of love between himself and his people. He was jealous of any other god who might draw away the love of Israel. Marital fidelity is frequently used in Scripture to portray God's covenant relationship with his people (e.g., Hosea; Eph. 5:21-33). The beauty of loving union with God and therefore also of a loving Christian marriage stand in sharp contrast to the horror of harlotry both religiously in idolatry and socially in broken marriage ties.

Blood is sacred (10-16). Blood stood for life. Shedding of blood was therefore a heinous offence – God alone gave life and he alone could take it away. Blood could not therefore be used for mere human consumption, but God had appointed that it was 'the blood that makes atonement, by reason of the life'. Atonement is God's initiative and it is achieved by outpoured life. Purification and the forgiveness of sins depend upon the shedding of blood (Heb. 9:22). Sacrificial death is required for redemption. And now, as Andrew Bonar points out in his Banner of Truth commentary, we 'must live by blood' (John 6:53-56).

The prohibitions concerning blood were so fundamental to the life of Israel that they were to be strictly observed not only by the Jews but also by all foreigners living in their midst (10,12). Even the Council of Jerusalem insisted on this for the early Gentile Christians (Acts 15:20,29).

THOUGHT: Atonement is God's initiative and it is achieved by outpoured blood.

18 Sexual purity

The basis of a moral purity lies not in mere humanitarian ethics, but in the nature of Yahweh, Israel's God (2,30). This chapter not only lists a variety of negatives, but stresses the positive rock-like foundation of his ordinances and statutes (4,26). His will is morally good, is acceptable to his followers and is incomparably perfect (Rom. 12:2). The land had vomited out its previous inhabitants because of their sexual immorality (25), and Israel was warned against similar sin leading to the same fate (28, compare Amos 2).

The negative prohibitions of this chapter range around various forms of incest (6-18) and perversion (19-23) with the threat that defilement brings judgement (24-30).

1. Incest. Neither polygamy nor levirate marriage is forbidden in this chapter, but rather incestuous sexual relationships with close members of the family. Sexual intercourse with a *living* brother's wife was forbidden (16), although the ancient levirate marriage custom continued to be valid (Gen. 38; Deut. 25:5-10; Matt. 22:23-33). The sad history of Jacob adds strength to v. 18 and the dread word 'rival'.

2. Perversion. Purposeful breaking of 15:24 is now categorised (19) with adultery (20), conformity with the practices of Molech (21), homosexuality (22) and bestial sexual perversion (23). It is clear that children were burned as living sacrifices to Molech, but the words 'by fire' are not in the Hebrew and this verse is in the context of sexual aberrations. It is more likely that it refers to the practice of giving children to shrine authorities to be trained as temple prostitutes. Such sin by God's chosen people brought contempt on his name, whereas the election and purposes of God are for the sake of his name (e.g. Ezek. 20:9,14,22,44). The total condemnation of homosexual acts is repeated in Lev. 20:13 and further castigated in Rom. 1:26,27. Like homosexuality, bestial sex was evidently common in the surrounding nations and is utterly condemned (e.g. Exod. 22:19; Deut. 27:21).

Righteousness and sin affect the nature both of man and of his environment (24-30). The original righteousness of man at Creation was mirrored in the glories of the Garden of Eden; the Fall included a curse on the ground. Here also, in Leviticus 18, it is seen that sin defiles the land and to this day the whole of creation is 'subjected to futility' and is 'groaning in travail' as it waits to be 'set free' in the final consummation of redemption (Rom. 8:19-23).

THOUGHT FOR TODAY: Israel was warned not to follow the example and standards of surrounding heathen society. This warning remains a constantly valid and relevant word (Rom. 12:2).

19 A miscellany of ordinances

Some critics maintain that this chapter is a hotch-potch of ordinances from a variety of sources which have all been jumbled up together. This assumption may not be to our taste, but certainly it is impossible to find any clear-cut order in the chapter. There are representative ordinances from virtually every classification of commandment, so that it may truly be said that this chapter represents the Law in miniature. However there is one central theme, the holy nature of the Lord: the refrain 'I am the Lord' runs through the whole chapter. We note again the fundamental biblical truth that man's holiness depends ultimately on a true relationship with a holy God (2).

It is noteworthy that the specific commandments begin with a right relationship with one's parents and then a rejection of all idolatry (3,4). Reverence for parents is further expanded with the command to respect and honour the old (32). The strict opposition to all forms of idolatry includes absolute prohibition of all occult practices and the consultation of mediums or wizards (26,31). Verses 27 and 28 also seem to be related to heathen practices. The positive counterpart to the negative prohibition of idolatry is that the Lord shall be first in every aspect of daily life; thus fruit shall be given to the Lord before it may be harvested for human consumption (23-25).

Great emphasis is placed on righteous social relationships in which justice reigns. The Israelite was not to take advantage of the defenceless (13,14), while justice and testimony were to be totally impartial (15,16). It is interesting that partiality was not even allowed when it favoured the poor; this disallows any modern philosophy which encourages anything that benefits the oppressed. Justice stands above all class, social or economic distinction. But constant care for the welfare of the poor was obligatory (9,10). Thus the key to social well-being is 'you shall love your neighbour as yourself' (18) – this is a better philosophy than the hatred of class warfare or the selfish greed of unbridled capitalism. This love for the defenceless foreigner and for the poor is reinforced by the reminder that Israel, too, had been oppressed strangers in the land of Egypt and had been delivered by the God whose commands they were obeying (36) – care for and salvation of the oppressed is a vital part of the very nature of Yahweh.

20 Further miscellaneous ordinances

In essence this chapter has many of the same ordinances as the previous one, but each set of prohibitions is taken a step further – offering of children to Molech (1-5), consulting mediums and wizards (6,27), reverence of parents (9), sexual relationships (10-21), distinguishing between the clean and the unclean (25).

In the context of personal and national holiness the initiative lay in God's hands. He it was who sanctified Israel (8) and had separated them from other peoples (24). 'Sanctifies' is intimately related to the concept of separation. Israel was separated from heathen nations because she was set apart for the service of the Lord and for an intimate relationship with him. Because of this high calling she was to be holy in the sense of morally righteous. This righteousness was not only to be in the personal life of each individual, but was to be displayed also in a national life of justice. Israel's responsibilities were clear, but still it was God who sanctified and separated. It was also God who would judge the wicked and cut them off; and it was he who would give Israel the promised land 'flowing with milk and honey' (24).

Judgement would strike the guilty and also those who condoned sin by 'hiding their eyes from that man' (4). Neither family unity nor national cohesion allowed sin to be condoned. The cult of Molech was such an abomination that it could not be allowed any foothold in God's people. Often Israel was tempted to practise heathen rites in the name of Yahweh and then syncretism flourished (e.g. Exod. 32:4,5; Judges 17). God's judgement was therefore radical – 'cut them off' (3,5,6, etc.), 'stone him' (2,27), 'put to death' (2,4,9,10,15), 'burned with fire' (14), 'die childless' (20,21). Contamination could not be allowed to permeate the people and continue from generation to generation. Sadly, however, all these precautions failed to preserve Israel's purity – the heart of man is incorrigible without the redemption of Christ and the renewal of the Holy Spirit.

Questions for further study and discussion on Leviticus 16–20

1. Work through Hebrews to see its use of the word blood. What are the parallels with the Day of Atonement in Leviticus 16?

2. What do Leviticus 16 and 17 teach about sin and cleansing from sin? What does this teach us about what Jesus accomplished when he died on the cross?

3. The Israelites added Canaanite religious practices to their worship. What forms of syncretism are current today? How can we guard against absorbing, consciously or unconsciously, the ideas of non-Christian philosophies and religions (compare Rom. 12:2)?

4. How would you answer the argument that Leviticus 18 and 20 are no longer relevant, and all sexual relationships are good and acceptable if motivated by 'true love'?

5. How would you answer the question, 'How can I become holy?' (Lev. 20)?

6. What occult activities are present in society today? In the light of biblical teaching, what should the Christian's attitude be?

7. Look at the teaching on social justice in chapter 19. In what ways are these commandments broken today? Suggest practical ways in which the church can demonstrate God's demand for social justice.

8. What does Leviticus 20 teach about God's judgement? What does the New Testament say about judgement?

21 Priestly purity

The chapter divides easily into three sections. In the first (1-9) the undefiled holiness of the priesthood is commanded. This is further developed by the final verses (16-24) in which it is ordained that no one could become a priest if he had any physical deformity or blemish. Sandwiched between these two sections on the priesthood comes a passage enjoining even stricter holiness on the high priest (10-15). Each section has one key word – 'holy' (6,7,8), 'anointing oil' (10,12) and 'blemish' (17,18,21,23).

1. Holy. The constant refrain of the Pentateuch is holiness. The priest was to be holy unto God (6,7). The emphasis was on the almighty God rather than the covenant-making Yahweh. The priest was also to be holy unto the people of Israel (8). The man of God had to set an example of purity and holiness in the midst of God's people. He was not to become too intimately involved in death and mourning, for death had a ritually defiling character. He could make an exception for his close relatives (2,3) whereas the high priest was not to have association with any dead body, even that of his own parents (11). The Hebrew text of v.4 is unclear, but it clearly does not mean he was not to mourn his wife, for Ezekiel's case was evidently exceptional (Ezek. 24:16).

The priest's holiness was further maintained through marriage only to a virgin (7) and through the avoidance of gross immorality by his children (9). The early church continued this emphasis on a well ordered and disciplined household as a necessary condition for spiritual leadership (1 Tim. 3:4,5) for it is a basic principle in the eyes of God (compare God's dealings with Eli, 1 Sam. 2:12-17,22-25; 3:10-14). The priest's holiness of course also meant a careful separation from all signs of heathen worship (5).

2. Anointing oil. Anointing oil speaks to us both of royalty and of the sacrificial priestly function. It is not surprising then that the fulfilment of Israel's calling and hope was found in the Messiah, the anointed One. He is the royal Son of David and the perfect High Priest (Heb. 7:26). No mere human high priest could fulfil the perfect demands of utter holiness (e.g. v.10 and Mark 14:63), but Jesus is our uniquely perfect Messiah.

3. Blemish. As with the sacrificial animals, so also with the sacrificial priest, there had to be no physical blemish. This is surely a sign of that total moral and spiritual purity which was ultimately fulfilled in Jesus Christ.

22 More about priests and offerings

In the Levitical Law there was a clear separation between priest and people as well as between priest and that which had been dedicated to the service of God (2). In Jesus Christ these barriers are broken down, for the sacrificer is one with the sacrifice and he is also one with his people who are consecrated to his service (e.g. John 17:23). For the Christian there is no longer a sacrificing priesthood and therefore no clear-cut distinction between priest and people. The whole Christian community is called to be a 'holy priesthood, to offer spiritual sacrifices' (1 Peter 2:5). We have different functions, but we are all one in our fundamental calling to be priests of God.

However, the Levitical priest had to preserve his separation. Holy things were not to be contaminated by contact with outsiders. The priest's food could only be eaten by himself and his immediate family – visitors or hired servants were not considered part of the household (10). We see here the importance of the family and household in Jewish life.

How striking to our ears is the expression 'the bread of your God' (25)! Do we react by objecting that God does not need human bread? The objection has validity, but still he enjoys and is pleased by our human offerings, although he does not need them. How beautiful that mere man can bring pleasure and joy to Almighty God!

Again we are reminded in v.32 of the fundamental purpose in all these ordinances. It has been said again and again, but repetition is a biblical way of underlining importance. The aim here is that God might be hallowed among his people (32). And then the heathen nations around will see God's glory in his people and will also be attracted to him (e.g. Zech. 8:20-23 and Matt. 5:16). The basis as always was the redemptive activity of God which made it possible for man to enter into personal relationship with God and to know him as the covenant Lord (32). The whole teaching of Christ and the New Testament assumes the background of these great principles of the Pentateuch.

THOUGHT: The aim is that God might be hallowed among his people . . . then the nations around will see God's glory in his people and will also be attracted to him.

23 The sacred calendar

Israel's year was marked by sacred feasts which became a divine method of repeated teaching. Such a system has the danger of becoming a legalistic routine (Col. 2:16), but its virtue is that it refreshes the memory concerning God's gracious dealings with his people. Evangelicals have sometimes reacted against oft-repeated visual teaching in the form of special days or rituals, but God constantly used such approaches.

The first and perhaps the most important feast was the weekly Sabbath, a day of 'solemn rest' (3). The Sabbath was to be a day 'to the Lord' (3) in which he was to be central. The second aspect of the Sabbath was the cessation of work and the enjoyment of rest (3). The Sabbath was not merely a day of negative prohibitions, for it was primarily a feast day.

A wealth of memories from Israel's history invade the mind as one progresses through this list of feasts: Passover, Unleavened Bread, First Fruits, Pentecost, Atonement and finally the Feast of Booths. Each in turn is to have yet greater significance in its fulfilment in Christ who is our passover lamb and the first fruits of our future resurrection (1 Cor. 15:20-23). In the past there were the redemptive events of Israel's liberation from Egypt (42,43), and in the future there would be the climax of the gift of the Spirit of Christ at Pentecost while still to come there is the prospect of the culmination of our hope at Jesus' coming again. The Spirit is the earnest of the yet greater salvation which shall be ours.

In the midst of cataloguing the glorious and solemn feasts Leviticus breaks off to include a further brief reminder of social responsibility for the poor and the stranger (22). At the heart of all the feasts was God's grace and salvation for otherwise hopeless men. It is therefore not irrelevant that these verses stress again Israel's obligation to show grace to the defenceless. The stranger had no tribe or family to defend and care for him, so he was as easily oppressed as the poor.

The feasts were not only visual aids for teaching; they were also an opportunity for Israel to 'give to the Lord' (37,38). In fact v.37 states that the aim of these solemn religious gatherings was 'for presenting to the Lord offerings'. What joy it was for the people of Israel to meet for the religious feasts and together pour out all their gifts, votive offerings and freewill offerings!

24 Unbroken homage

The light (1-4). This stands in Leviticus not for outgoing witness, but for the continual practice of prayer and worship. Presumably the people were to be engaged in worship during the day, but while they slept the light was kept burning 'from evening to morning' (3). The New Testament further developed the idea of light. Jesus is the light of the world and Christians are also called to let their light shine. In the Old Testament Israel's light was 'in the tent of meeting' (3). The Gentile nations might be drawn in like moths to the light (Isa. 60:3), but Israel's light was not an evangelistic mission. The church, however, faces an outgoing commission in which her light is not to be kept to herself (Matt. 5:14-16).

The bread of the Presence (5-9). Israel, in the person of the priests, was invited to share in a feast before the Lord on a table of pure gold (6). All twelve tribes were represented (6). This foreshadows the Messianic banquet in the Kingdom in which all nations shall share. When we take part together in the Lord's Supper, we look back to these priestly feasts and to the Passover meal; we also look forward to their climax in glory. As with the light, so therefore now with the bread of the Presence, there is a missionary significance. Let our light shine outwards to all nations and let us invite everyone to enter God's community so that they may share in the feast.

Human failure (10-23). Our missionary purpose is that the name of the Lord should be glorified, loved and worshipped. Sadly this name has been cursed and blasphemed (11,16). What grace that God continues to use weak and sinful instruments to spread the glory of his name despite our failure throughout the course of history. Abraham followed his call (Gen. 12:3) with despicable behaviour in Egypt (Gen. 12:10-16) and this was typical of the whole history of Israel until the perfect Israelite came to be the light of the world and to be the bread of life.

We note that sin came through a mixed marriage and, true to type, in the tribe of Dan (compare Judges 17 and 18). But the judgement was not hasty and ill-considered (12).

The law of an eye for an eye (17-20) improved on indiscriminate retribution, but Jesus replaced personal desire for rigid justice with a new law of love (Matt. 5:38-48).

FEAST	DATES	PRINCIPAL REFERENCES
Passover	14 Nisan (March/April)	Exodus 12;13 Deuteronomy 16:1-8 Numbers 28:16-25 1 Corinthians 5:7 Leviticus 23:4-8
Weeks/Firstfruits/ Harvest Pentecost	6 Sivan (May/June) 50 days after Passover	Exodus 23:16a Numbers 28:26-31 Deuteronomy 16:9-12 Leviticus 23:15-22
Tabernacles Ingathering	15 Tishri (Sept/Oct)	Exodus 23:16b Leviticus 23:33-43 Numbers 29:12-40
Day of Atonement	10 Tishri (Sept/Oct)	Exodus 30:10 Leviticus 16;23:26-32 Numbers 29:7-11 Hebrews 9;10
Trumpets	1 Tishri (Sept/Oct)	Leviticus 23:23-25 Numbers 29:1-6

MAIN FEATURES	SIGNIFICANCE
Possibly originally some nomad festival but clearly linked with the Exodus from Egypt. Unleavened bread was probably originally a separate feast but later merged. Originally a meal of roast lamb and bitter herbs eaten in families with a recitation of Exodus event. Later centralised at the central shrine, ultimately the Jerusalem Temple. Unleavened bread was to be eaten for seven days.	Served as a reminder of the saving act of God. Eating unleavened bread originally acted as a reminder of the urgency of the escape. Later leaven came to be seen as a symbol of sin and so the removal of leaven from the house spoke of purification and separation from sin. The New Testament sees Christ as the ultimate fulfilment of the Passover – his death redeeming his people from bondage to sin.
A harvest thanksgiving at the end of the barley harvest. A day free of work, involving a freewill offering from the harvest together with animal sacrifices (Leviticus and Numbers differ on details) and cereal offerings.	A celebration of God's provision marked by joy and gratitude. The animal sacrifices served as a reminder of men's sinfulness and therefore unworthiness of God's gifts. Also linked with an injunction to care for the poor and needy.
A harvest thanksgiving at the end of the fruit harvest in which the people lived for seven days in shelters made of branches. The first and eighth days were work free. Animal sacrifices and cereal offerings were made each day.	A further joyous celebration of God's goodness and man's dependence. The leaf shelters acted as a special reminder of the time in the wilderness.
Day of penitence and fasting. Sacrifice of bull (sin offering for the priesthood) and goat (for people). Blood sprinkled in the holy place. Second goat driven out into the wilderness.	Demonstrates that man in his sin cannot come to God but that God will restore the relationship where there is repentance and trust. The New Testament sees the ritual fulfilled in Christ whose sacrificial death provides the means whereby we may be accepted by God.
Day of rest. Animal sacrifices and cereal offerings.	Possibly at some time a New Year festival. The trumpets may have been a reminder that God was the leader of his people.

25 Sabbatical year and Jubilee

Once again it is interesting to observe the close connection between people and land. Both were to keep their sabbath. This chapter teaches a sabbatical year every seven years (1-7) and also a Jubilee Year after 49 years. The former was carefully kept throughout the centuries of Israel's history. Nehemiah 10:31 refers to this and later the Jewish historian Josephus alludes several times to the sabbatical year. There is no evidence, however, that the Jubilee Year was ever kept, although some of its basic principles were never forgotten.

In the wilderness, in the double provision of manna on the day before the sabbath, God had provided for Israel's needs during the sabbath. Now he promised adequate supply of crops to allow for the observance of the sabbatical year (18-22). Israel had to learn that God can be trusted to provide our needs if we obey him.

The land of Canaan belonged to God and he divided it amongst the various families of Israel. Land was therefore a divine and inalienable gift. There could be no permanent sale of land, for it would revert to its original God-chosen owner at the Jubilee. This cancellation of debts and return of family heritages made large-scale inequalities almost impossible and always temporary. The prophets kept alive this vision of God's hatred of gross inequalities in land distribution with its often attendant problem of abiding debt.

Some theologians today (e.g. J. Yoder in *The Politics of Jesus*) hold that the egalitarian principles of justice in the institution of the Jubilee Year are a vital part of Jesus' message and work of salvation. Yoder sees this particularly in the Gospel of Luke with its specific emphasis on universal mission. Thus in Luke 4:18,19 Jesus' ministry to the poor includes 'to set at liberty those who are oppressed' in the context of 'the acceptable year of the Lord'.

Israel's salvation from Egypt (38,42,55) meant they were never again to be slaves – except to the Lord himself (55). Paul, too, delights to start many of his letters with the words 'I, Paul, a slave of Jesus Christ'.

Houses (as opposed to family land) could be permanently sold within a walled city, but in a village the house was considered part of the land. Such irrevocable sales included a safety clause – the house could be redeemed at any time during the first year after sale.

Family care and responsibility remained, despite all financial predicaments (35-49). It remains equally vital in the Christian church among brothers in Christ.

26 A concluding charge to Israel

The final two chapters summarise God's commandments to Israel (46 and 27:34). As in the Ten Commandments, so here the basis lay in a right worship of God (1) which would be evidenced by the keeping of the sabbath and a reverence for God's sanctuary (2).

God promised that obedience to his statutes would result in his provision of peace (6), prosperity (4,5,9,10) and victory (7,8). But the climax of God's blessing parallels the idyllic picture of his relationship with Adam and Eve before the Fall – 'I will make my abode among you' (11), 'I will walk among you' (12). This is the result of a peaceful and righteous relationship with God and is the answer to the modern quest for freedom and dignity in human existence – 'I have broken the bars of your yoke and made you walk erect' (13). Note the reiterated emphasis on God as the agent of blessing through the repeated use of 'I'.

Promises are balanced by threats. The justice of God inevitably meant judgement if Israel spurned his ordinances. The chapter unfolds a growing cataclysm of tragedy. Disregard for God's judgements led to ever greater calamity. The fearful nature of God's judgements is underlined by the repeated 'sevenfold' (18,21,24,28).

But God constantly looks for repentance, longing for Israel to 'hearken' (14,21,27). He looks for confession of sin (40), a humbling of heart and making amends (41). Then comes God's promise of renewed covenant relations, for God never forgot his covenant promises to Israel's patriarchal fathers (42-45). Although God will forgive and renew, he still demands righteous judgement for sin. Israel would still suffer banishment from the land and exile in enemy lands (43,44), so that the land could gain its designated sabbath rest despite Israel's failure to observe this commandment (43).

In contrast to the peace and dignity of the righteous, sin in Israel would result in fear (e.g. 36), pining away (39) and such devastation that enemy nations 'shall be astonished' (32) – what a contrast to the concept of light in chapter 24!

THOUGHT: Sin not only affects our own well-being, but also discredits the name of the Lord in the eyes of those around us.

27 An appendix on valuations

Having summarised the basic spiritual principles of the Law in chapter 26, Leviticus now closes with some very practical details of its outworkings. Gifts vowed to the Lord needed to be valued if they were to be redeemed with money. Such vowed gifts could include people (1-8), animals (9-13), houses (14,15) or land (16-25).

Hannah's offering of the baby Samuel to the Lord was typical of a human offering by vow, while the example of Jephthah and his daughter (Judg. 11:29-40) demonstrates the then prevailing ignorance of the Levitical laws concerning the redemption of a vow.

The valuation of a person according to age and sex was economically realistic. The equal value of all men in the eyes of God has already been shown in Exodus 30:11-16.

Whereas family land reverted back to the original owners automatically and without payment at the Jubilee when it was in human possession, if it had been vowed to the Lord it needed to be redeemed. The fact that the original owners might not want to redeem it meant that priests could multiply their land ownership (21). Greed for wealth and power has always been a snare for those in positions of spiritual leadership.

What has been 'devoted' (21,28) may never be bought back. The word *herem* does not merely mean 'dedicate', but signifies something to be 'ruthlessly and completely destroyed' (Snaith). Joshua 6:17 is an example of this. That which is devoted belongs absolutely and irrevocably to God alone (28).

Tithing was practised long before the giving of the Law (e.g. Gen. 14:20 and 28:22), but because of misuse is only mentioned in a negative manner in the New Testament (Matt. 23:23). When God's direct kingship over Israel gave way to the institution of a human monarchy, the tithes were sometimes appropriated by the king (1 Sam. 8:15-17) – church history has further illustrated the danger of confusing spiritual and political leadership. However, misuse should never blind us to the validity of the principle of tithing. All our material and financial possessions belong to God; we acknowledge this by joyfully giving a representative portion to him and to his service through his ministers.

WARNING: Greed for wealth and power has always been a snare for those in positions of spiritual leadership.

Questions for further study and discussion on Leviticus 21–27

1. An ordered and disciplined household is 'a necessary condition for spiritual leadership' – see note on Leviticus 21 and 1 Timothy 3:4,5. Why is this so? What are the particular difficulties which face the homes of Christian leaders?

2. Christians are called to be priests of God (see note on Lev. 22). What does this mean?

3. What was the purpose of all God's commands (see Lev. 22:31,32)? In what ways does this challenge our own lives and the life of our churches?

4. Study the various feasts and their significance in chapter 23. What lessons can we learn for Christian worship today?

5. What principles of social justice may be deduced from the Jubilee Year, and how can these be applied to today's world?

6. List the blessings and judgements which result from obedience and disobedience in chapter 26. In what ways does this still apply today?

7. 'Greed for wealth and power has always been a snare for those in spiritual leadership' (see note on Lev. 27). How can we guard against this in our own lives? Make this a prayer topic for your spiritual leaders.

8. What can we learn of the character of God from these chapters?

Analysis of Numbers

33:50–36:13 The prospect of Canaan

1 The census

Just one month after the erection of the tabernacle of the tent of meeting (Exod. 40:2,17) arrangements were made for the oversight of the tabernacle by the Levites (47-53) and therefore their freedom from military responsibilities. The other eleven tribes were organised for the fighting needed in order to gain the promised land – this is the heart of the book of Numbers.

The numbering of Israel in this chapter was only of men and it excluded those under twenty. Its aim was that they might be divided into companies for military service (3). Gray (ICC Commentary on Numbers) suggests that 'all the tribal numbers are purely artificial' because they seem unlikely as they stand. However, he also points out that 'thousands' can mean 'clans' (as in v.16). Hundreds and thousands may refer to the nominal strength of military units.

2 Samuel 24 and 1 Chronicles 21 are sometimes quoted to demonstrate that it was wrong to number Israel and that therefore statistical research into the Christian church is also to be avoided. David's motives in his numbering of God's people were presumptuous. Likewise Christian statistics should have a God-glorifying motive rather than merely a triumphalistic view of the Church. D. McGavran (*Understanding Church Growth*) points out that without accurate numbering of God's people it is impossible to pastor effectively.

The Levites not only had the responsibility of looking after the tabernacle, but they also encamped around it (50,53) between the people of Israel and the presence of God's holiness. This shielding of the tabernacle was to prevent others approaching, for it is death to come as a sinner into contact with God. Paul therefore always reiterates the essential truth that as Christians we are 'in Christ'. Covered by the 'wedding garment' of Christ's righteousness we are now able to enter the presence of God.

Numbers catalogues the failures and disobedience of Israel in her wilderness wanderings, but the story starts well (54). Israel obeyed 'all that the Lord commanded Moses'. The minutely detailed laws and the emphasis on God's burning holiness were designed to teach the necessity of absolute obedience.

QUESTION: What use does your church make of statistics?

2 Israel in array

The key to this chapter is the centrality of the tent of meeting in the midst of the surrounding tribes. No longer was the tent of meeting outside the camp (Exod. 33:7), but was constantly in the very centre. This remained true whether Israel was on the march or encamped (2). God's presence was localised and visible. This was fulfilled in the visible incarnate presence of God in the person of Jesus Christ. Today God's presence is neither visible nor localised, for we cannot limit the Holy Spirit. However, the centrality of God is vital for his people in all ages.

The eleven non-Levitical tribes were placed around the tent of meeting. When encamped they faced inwards, thus always looking towards the presence of God. In the detailed disposition of the people we note the importance of careful organisation. No tribe has any position of privilege for only God is pre-eminent. The apostle James later attacked pride of position and partiality in God's church (Jas. 2:1-9). Jesus himself taught that Christian pride is in humble service rather than in privileged position (Mark 9:33-37; 10:35-45). The church needs constantly to be reminded of this, for pride and lust for status are ever-present temptations.

It seems that each tribe had its own 'ensign' while each group adopted the 'standard' of its leader (31). Tradition states that each tribe's ensign had on it a piece of cloth of the same colour as its stone in the high priest's breastplate (Exod. 28:21).

The structures of Israelite society reveal a balanced emphasis on the individual and on family and tribal cohesion. 'Every one' was located 'in his family', according to his 'fathers' house' (34). The Sri Lankan theologian L. De Silva says: 'To be is to be related. The individual exists through his relationship with others.' The relationships of the family and the larger social units are fundamental to human life. This is God's plan for us; it is not just an abstract sociological theory. Paul, too, places the Christian life within the context of relationships (Eph. 5:21–6:9).

3 The tribe of Levi

God had ordained that all the first-born of Israel should be dedicated to him. This dated back to his slaying of all Egypt's first-born and his salvation of Israel (13). Now God commanded that the Levites replace other first-born Israelites (45) and even the cattle of the Levites should be offered instead of other cattle. The redemption price of five shekels was to be paid for each first-born man above the number of the Levites (46-51). The presence of the Levites in the midst of the Israelite encampment was therefore a perpetual reminder of God's saving acts in Egypt and of the fact that Israel belonged to the Lord.

We note that the numbering of the Levites was not a military requirement as in chapter 1, but concerned the first fruits or first-born. Therefore every male 'from a month old and upward' was numbered (15).

Aaron had four sons, but two of them had been killed because of their disobedience (4). Eleazar and Ithamar took over the priestly responsibilities (Lev. 10:12). They were not involved in matters of structural upkeep, but had charge of the 'rites within the sanctuary' – compare Acts 6:2-4. Is this a useful principle for our churches today? Moses and Aaron with their families were encamped to the east of the tabernacle, guarding the entry to the tent of meeting. Death was the consequence if anyone else came near (38).

The Levites ministered for the whole people at the tabernacle and had responsibility for the 'furnishings of the tent of meeting' (8). This high calling was matched by a ministry of service to Aaron the priest (6). Once again we see the combination of privileged calling and a humble ministry of service.

The Kohathites followed immediately after the priest when Israel was marching. They had special responsibilities with the care of the holiest of the tabernacle furniture which could not be carried in mere carts (4:15; 7:9). It seems that a scribal error has changed one Hebrew letter and thus written 8,600 instead of the more correct 8,300 (compare v.39). Kidner says, 'the fact that the Amramites were already a clan (27) suggests that Amram was a distant rather than an immediate progenitor of Moses (Exod. 6:18,20)'. It could also be that there were two men called Amram. Recent archaeological discoveries point to the fact that many of the names in the Pentateuch were quite common.

4 The tribe of Levi (continued)

Controversy rages concerning the age at which a Levite could commence his ministry. The Hebrew here states the lower age limit to have been thirty, but the Septuagint says twenty-five in agreement with 8:24. However 8:24 refers to performing 'the work in the service of the tent of meeting', while our passage deals only with the labour of carrying the tabernacle. In 1 Chronicles 23:24 King David lowers the age limit to twenty. It would seem that Jesus delayed his ministry as prophet and priest until he was thirty.

Retirement from the levitical ministry was fixed at the age of fifty (38). It seems biblical and wise to determine the age of retirement for those in spiritual ministry. The Christian church might have gained a more lively and up-to-date image if it had observed this principle.

We notice in these chapters a carefully designated line of command from God to Moses to Aaron through to the various families (e.g. 27,28). Israel was a theocracy, not a democracy. Authority is biblical, although authoritarianism denotes an unbiblical pride. Within the delineated framework of authority each group of families had a specific area of responsibility which it was trusted to fulfil. Aaron and his sons had the task of commanding and overseeing the work, but they entrusted the carrying out of the work to those under them. Moses learned similar principles of leadership and delegation from his father-in-law Jethro (Exod. 18:13-27).

Autocracy without such trustful delegation is unbiblical. Carefully structured organisational patterns are 'according to the commandment of the Lord' (49) and are not inimical to the work of his Spirit.

Again in this chapter the emphasis is on holiness and therefore on the need to cover the ark of the testimony (5) and all the sacred utensils when they were being moved. The Levites were to carry the holy things, but Aaron and his sons were to prevent them from touching anything (15) or even looking at them (20). Such was the burning holiness that death was the consequence of contact.

Eleazar, the elder of Aaron's two surviving children, was entrusted with the holiest functions (16) while the younger Ithamar had charge of the ministries of the sons of the Gershonites and of Merari (28,33). Age involves seniority and responsibility.

TO THINK OVER: Carefully structured organisational patterns are 'according to the commandment of the Lord' and are not inimical to the work of his Spirit.

5 'None of us lives to himself'

In the first four verses the command to expel the unclean from the camp is reiterated (compare Lev. 13:45,46; 15; Num. 19:11-13), while unfaithfulness to God (5-10) and in the marriage relationship (11-31) forms the subject of the succeeding verses.

1-4. *'Their* camp, in the midst of which *I* dwell' (3). The community of God's people is human and very fallible, but because it is God's dwelling place holiness is mandatory. The repetition of 'the people of Israel did so' (4) underlines the fact of obedience.

5-10. The same Hebrew word is translated 'breaking faith' (6) and 'acts unfaithfully' (12,27). Our relationship with God closely parallels the marriage ties. These verses assume that doing wrong to another man (7) is equivalent to breaking faith with the Lord (6). Restitution is made firstly to the man we have wronged – not to the Lord directly unless the wronged man is dead and has no kinsman (8). True worship of God always means love and forgiveness towards men. Restitution to God was made through gifts to his priests for their use. Giving to God and to his ministers are virtually equivalent.

11-31. Gray in his ICC Commentary on Numbers comments that such trial by ordeal 'has innumerable analogies in practices generally prevalent in antiquity.' We note, however, that here it is the Lord who judged (16,18,21) through a potion which had in itself no potency. It was merely 'holy water' (17) mixed with dust from the floor of the tabernacle. The written words of the oath were washed off into this water (23) and the accused woman drank it.

There has been some debate about the exact meaning of the thigh falling away and the body swelling (27). Traditional Jewish interpretation has linked this to the principle of 'with what measure a man metes, it is measured to him' and therefore the Mishnah says 'with the thigh she commences her transgression, and afterwards with the belly: therefore the thigh shall be first smitten and then the belly' (Sotah 1:7ff).

This chapter assumes the authority of the husband (29) and only allows for the wife to be found guilty (31). The man may have suffered from his jealous spirit, but no provision is here made for any accusation against him nor for any recompense if his accusations were false. We rejoice in the New Testament development with the command to husbands to 'love your wives, as Christ loved the church' (Eph. 5:25).

6 The Nazirite vow

The law concerning the Nazirite divides into three clear sections. The basic requirements were to abstain from strong drink and all products of the vine, to leave the hair uncut and to remain free from defiling contact with the dead (2-8). This is followed by regulations concerning accidental defilement by the dead (9-12) and details of the offerings and ritual to mark the end of the period of the vow (13-21). In spite of the later example of Samson it was normal for the vow to be temporary (8,12,13) – do Acts 18:18 and 21:24 refer to such temporary Nazirite vows?

It seems clear that there is a link between the root of the Hebrew *n-z-r* and the word for 'separation' (3,5, etc.) and 'consecration' (11,18, etc.). Thus the Nazirite was set apart in a special way for God. This passage is also relevant to the Christian, for the words 'saint' and 'sanctify' have something of the same meaning. However the call of the Christian is life-long, not temporary. Some preachers have linked the fact that Jesus came from Nazareth to the Nazirite vow, but this has no basis. It is possible (although debatable) that John the Baptist may have been a Nazirite, but Jesus drank of the fruit of the vine (John 2) and also had contact with the dead (Luke 7:14; John 11). It is vain to insist on abstinence from alcoholic drinks as a mark of true discipleship while objecting to men having long hair!

The presence of Nazirites in Israel's midst was a constant reminder of God's call to holiness. The Nazirite was specially 'holy to the Lord' (8). God himself calls some men to this act of consecration (Amos 2:11) and it is therefore a fearful sin to cause them to stumble (Amos 2:12). The holiness of the vow was further demonstrated by the detailed ritual and considerable offerings required on completion of the period of the vow (13-20).

The threefold repetition of the Lord's name in the Aaronic blessing (22-27) ensured the placing of that name upon the people of Israel. This not only guaranteed God's presence and gracious blessing but also sealed Israel's position as the possession of the Lord. The blessing assumed material benefits and the even greater peace of the Lord's face shining joyfully upon his people.

Questions for further study and discussion on Numbers 1–6

1. The central tent of meeting was God's practical way of demonstrating his centrality in the life of the people (Num. 2). Discuss practical ways in which we can keep God central in our lives. What suggestions does the New Testament make?

2. 'To be is to be related' (see note on Num. 2). What groups of people are lonely in the area where you live? In what ways is – or could – your church reaching out to help them?

3. In what ways did Jesus demonstrate the primacy of humble service (see note on Num. 2, and also Phil. 2:5-11)? How would you define humility? Modern society judges people according to their status and the job they do. Is this true of people in the church? How can it be avoided?

4. What is the difference between authority and authoritarianism (note on Num. 4)?

5. Some churches suffer because authority is kept in the hands of a few people, instead of being delegated (Num. 4). Why do you think this happens? Discuss ways in which your church and church groups should and could follow the principles of delegation (compare Acts 6:1-6). What principles of Christian leadership and of organisational patterns for the church may be learned from these chapters?

6. Study further the biblical development of the marriage imagery for the relationship between God and his people. In this context think of the meaning of 'breaking faith' (5:6) and 'jealousy' (5:14).

7. How can 'separation' (6:5) be reconciled to relevant involvement in society?

8. Study carefully each phrase of the Aaronic blessing (6:24-26) and consider further the significance of the phrase 'so shall they put my name upon the people of Israel' (6:27).

7 The best for God

What a glorious succession of events! Firstly there was the final anointing and consecration of the tabernacle and all its contents with special emphasis on the altar and its utensils (1), then twelve days of particular offerings from the representatives of the twelve tribes of Israel (12-88). These twelve days were presumably interrupted by a Sabbath's rest and thus led immediately to the climactic celebration of the first Passover since Israel left Egypt (Num. 9:2,3).

Emphasis on the supremacy of God's holy presence through the consecration of the tabernacle led naturally to joyful and voluntary giving (2-10) both on the day of the anointing and dedication of the altar and also during the ensuing twelve days. This joyful succession of offerings found its culmination in the solemn celebration of the Passover Feast when the people of Israel feasted together in remembrance of God's merciful salvation from slavery and degradation. The overriding impression of this chapter is therefore one of spontaneous liberality in the context of God's saving grace.

Why did the sons of Merari receive twice as many wagons and oxen as the sons of Gershon? The Gershonites were more numerous than the sons of Merari (Num. 3:22,34) and their work apparently equally onerous (4:21-33). The answer may lie in the repetition of the words 'according to their service' (7,8). The Kohathites received no wagons or oxen because they carried the holy things on their shoulders (9).

Moses' intention on entering the tent of meeting was to 'speak with' the Lord (89). His actual experience was that he heard the voice of God 'speaking to' him. Dialogue with God should inevitably result in more hearing than speaking. God originally commissioned Moses for leadership of Israel with audible words (Exod. 3:4). Samuel (1 Sam. 3:4) and Paul (Acts 26:14) enjoyed the same experience. The voice came from 'above the mercy seat that was upon the ark of the testimony' – God is not contained in or limited by the outward symbols of his presence. Likewise he is not bound always to speak to his people either with audible utterance or in any other manner.

THOUGHT: Dialogue with God should inevitably result in more hearing than speaking.

8 The living light

In Leviticus 24:1-4 we observed the vital significance of the golden lampstand and the light. The number seven shows the glorious perfection of the light which was later to be seen in its fullness in the person of Jesus who is the light of the world. His illuminating glory is the culmination of history (Rev. 21:22-24; 22:5). The apostle John was particularly impressed by the concept of light. He starts his Gospel with the light of God coming into the world in the person of the incarnate Jesus and likewise his first letter develops the theme that 'God is light' (1:5) and therefore we must 'walk in the light' (1:7). The Levitical lampstand with all its beautiful workmanship in gold gave way to the yet more glorious light of Jesus, so the Temple and all its contents became redundant and were duly destroyed in AD 70.

God consecrated to himself 'all the first-born among the people of Israel' (17). The Levites were consecrated to the Lord in their place (18). At their dedication the whole people of Israel had to 'lay their hands on the Levites' (10) to make the Levites their representatives as an offering to the Lord. The Levites then laid their hands upon the heads of the sacrificial bulls (12) which were offered as sin and burnt offerings for the atonement of the Levites and thus also for all Israel. The New Testament develops this theme of substitutionary atonement. Jesus Christ died for us and in our place to make atonement for us.

The consecration of the Levites was composed of various significant elements – cleansing through the sprinkling of water, the shaving off of all hair, washing of the body and clothes, presentation of cereal, sin and burnt offerings before the Lord and the laying on of hands by the whole people of Israel; Aaron offered the Levites before the Lord 'as a wave offering from the people of Israel, that it may be theirs to do the service of the Lord' (11). It is no light calling to serve the Lord as representatives of his people. We notice that the initiative in the call to Levitical service was firmly in God's hands: he commanded Moses who in turn directed Aaron. They, together with the people of Israel, did to the Levites (20) what God had ordained.

9:1–10:10 Worshippers, pilgrims, warriors

The second Passover (1-14). The trauma of Egypt came vividly to mind as Israel partook of the Passover feast 'in the wilderness' (1,5), but joyful remembrance of God's salvation predominated. 'In the evening' (3) further reminds us of the institution and celebration of the Lord's Supper which likewise looks back to God's deliverance from enslaving bonds. In both cases the feast is a remembrance.

Moses' meekness before the Lord is demonstrated by his patient waiting on the Lord for his directions (8). The Law seemed clear although somewhat relentless in the case of uncleanness through contact with a dead body. It would have been only too easy for Moses to declare the Law without consulting the Lord. God's gracious decision (10) typifies his loving mercy to his children. He extends kindness to those who truly seek him, but unbending judgement and wrath abide on the man who wilfully neglects his ordinances and refrains from the Passover (13).

God's salvation was not only for the Jew, but also for any one who would join his people and therefore keep the Passover 'to the Lord' (14). In God's saving love there is neither Jew nor Gentile. This basic message forms the heart of much New Testament teaching. The Kingdom of the one universal God is for all nations – Jews, Samaritans, Gentiles, unto the uttermost parts of the earth.

The cloud and fire (15-23). What an idyllic picture of a people under the clear guidance of the Lord! All their movements were 'at the command of the Lord' (18,23). If the cloud remained static over the tabernacle for a few days, Israel was content to await God's time to move. The Christian covets such assurance that the Lord is moving him on or requiring him to continue where he is. We desire to move through life under the leadership and guidance of the Lord's presence.

The silver trumpets (10:1-10). The two silver trumpets seem to have had a dual function. Firstly they served to call the whole congregation or their leaders (3,4) and to blow an alarm (5,6). Secondly, in time of war the alarm was sounded to summon the Lord's mighty aid to the end that 'you shall be saved from your enemies' (9). Likewise at feasts the trumpets called upon the Lord to join his people by his presence (10).

10:11-36 As an army with banners

Israel had been encamped at Sinai for almost a year (11; compare Exod. 19:1); the Law had been given with all its patterns of worship and community life. God was now ready to lead his people forward. Imagine Israel's sense of excitement as 'the cloud was taken up' (11) and they 'set out for the first time' (13)! The order of marching was well defined (Num. 2) as also was the procedure for the carrying of the holy things. Doubtless the silver trumpets of the preceding verses thrilled Israel in their summons to march.

Moses invited his Gentile father-in-law to share Israel's fortunes (29-32). Contrast the case of Ruth! Moses trusted the Lord's leadership, but still he recognised his need for expert desert-trained 'eyes' (31). Faith and human means often work together. It seems from Judges 4:11 that Hobad did not separate himself from Israel. Here he is said to be a Midianite, whereas Judges 4:11 talks of the Kenites. Both were nomadic Arab tribes and interrelationship may have existed through marriage.

Gentiles who joined themselves to Israel shared in Yahweh's blessings (compare 9:14). During the course of her history the prospering of Israel at the hands of God attracted various Gentiles; this became the longing dream of the prophets (e.g. Zech. 8:20-23) and was partly fulfilled in the coming of Gentile wise men, the Canaanite woman, the Greeks and even the Roman centurion, to Jesus. The final fulfilment in the Kingdom will see a great multitude from all tribes and nations worshipping before the throne and before the Lamb (Rev. 7:9-17).

God's mighty victorious leadership of his people and his gracious presence in their midst formed the basis of Moses' assurance as Israel set out (35,36). These verses are further developed in Psalm 68 with its exuberant joy at the Lord's grace and deliverance. Read Psalm 68 in this context and rejoice! Note here that once again Gentiles share in bringing gifts and worship to the Lord (Ps. 68:29,31,32). Moses did not desire the destruction of all the Gentile nations they would meet in their march into Canaan, but only those 'that hate thee', 'thy enemies' (35). Slaughter in the Old Testament is not wanton but is judgement of the corrupt and rotten.

FOR WORSHIP: Blessed be the Lord,
                   Who daily bears us up;
                   God is our salvation.
                   (Ps. 68:19)

The route of the Exodus

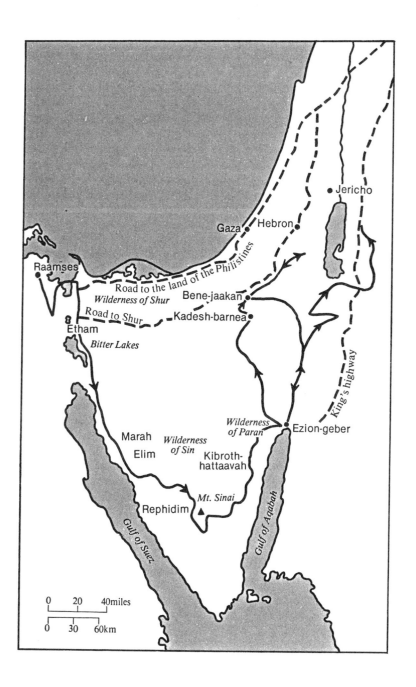

Jericho

Gaza • Hebron

Raamses

Road to the land of the Philistines

Wilderness of Shur

Bene-jaakan

Road to Shur — Kadesh-barnea

Etham

Bitter Lakes

King's highway

Wilderness of Paran • Ezion-geber

Marah   Wilderness
             of Sin
Elim   Kibroth-
                       hattaavah

Mt. Sinai

Rephidim

Gulf of Suez

Gulf of Aqabah

| 0 | 20 | 40miles |

| 0 | 30 | 60km |

11 Grumbling and God's reaction

Israel's complaints. The previous chapter left us with an excited sense of anticipation as Israel marched forward with the manifest leadership of her divine King. But Israel included an influential rabble element (4). Discontent, grumbling and covetous desire for more were marks of that sinful rabble influence (compare 1 Cor. 10:6-13). Israel forgot the pain of the past, remembering only the fish and other foods which were unlikely to be available in the desert. They despised the Lord's gracious provision of manna day by day.

God reacted to Israel's complaints with wrathful fire (1,10,33) and answered their materialistic prayers with an excess of quails. Too much even of a good thing nauseates. But God's judgement was not only through a surfeit of quails; his anger blazed forth in a plague (33). The first manifestation of God's wrath was placated by Moses' prayer (2), but there is no evidence that Moses prayed for relief from the plague of quails.

Moses' complaints. The lonely burden of leadership became intolerable. Moses was sensitive to criticism and complained that 'they weep before me' (13), whereas the grumbling was actually 'in the hearing of the Lord' (1,18). Excessive unshared responsibility easily leads to breakdown – 'the burden is too heavy for me' (14) – and can even invite suicidal tendencies (15).

God's answer was shared leadership through delegation. In Exodus this came about through the wise counsel of Jethro (Exod. 18:13-27). Are the seventy elders (16) the same men as those in Exodus 24:9-11? It would seem likely.

Moses learned his lesson. Jealousy of those under him who exercised spiritual gifts became unnecessary (28,29). In his meekness he longed that 'all the Lord's people were prophets' under the ministry of the Lord's Spirit (29). His leadership was not threatened by this.

The choice of the seventy was marked by the anointing of the Spirit (25) with the accompanying sign of prophecy. This initial gift was not permanent – 'they did so no more'.

Moses' second objection involved a cynical doubting of God's ability to feed the hosts of Israel (21-23). The depression that may result from loneliness and overwork can bring with it an apparent breakdown of faith. God's answer (23) is deeply encouraging and has strengthened Christians' faith through the ages. God's word is powerfully effective (Isa. 55:11) and it is personal in application – 'my word will come true for you' (23).

12 Disunity at the top

Moses' lack of jealousy (11:29) is now contrasted with the attitude of Miriam and Aaron. They enjoyed high privilege and position, but still coveted Moses' supreme leadership. Evidently it was Miriam who instigated the whispering campaign against Moses – her name is mentioned first (1) and she alone was punished (10). Was she jealous of Moses' wife? Moses' marriage with a foreigner formed the excuse for their rebellion, but the real cause was clearly jealousy of Moses and a desire for equal status with him. In cases of disagreement or schism we should be wise to discern the true hidden motives rather than taking words at face value.

The Hebrew *Cush* generally refers to Ethiopia, but it may also be used of the Cassites east of Babylonia. More likely in this case is Winckler's suggestion that the Cushites were a north Arabian people. This suits other passages where Moses' wife is said to be a Midianite (10:29) or Kenite (Judg. 1:16).

Moses' meekness was exemplary. It was God, not Moses, who took the initiative in countering this disunity (4). Aaron wrongly assumed, however, that the divine punishment was Moses' responsibility (11). The meek Moses was duly exalted. The Lord demonstrated his absolute trust in Moses and the prophetic privilege he bestows upon his servant (6-8). What a picture of intimate relationship with God! But Hebrews shows that the high calling of Moses is further proof of Jesus' incomparable superiority (Heb. 3:2,3).

Old Testament concepts of prophecy are closely related to the idea of seeing visions and dreaming dreams (6). God is not restricted in his ways of speaking to his people.

God's grace matched Aaron's repentance (11) and Moses' forgiving prayer (13). So Miriam was forgiven. God insisted, however, that forgiveness should not preclude some punishment in the form of a week's ritual uncleanness (14,15). Spitting in the face seems to have been a common expression of disgust (Deut. 25:9; Job 30:10; Isa. 50:6).

As in Leviticus 13, the disease with which Miriam was afflicted was clearly not what we today call 'leprosy', but there remains the symbolic significance of sin and therefore the need to shut her out of the camp. God, Moses and the people of Israel graciously waited the necessary seven days before resuming their march (15).

QUESTION: What can we learn from Moses' attitude throughout this incident?

13 Spying out the land

God does not expect blind faith. Commitment to his calling includes a careful assessment of the situation. God wanted all Israel to know both the likely rewards and the inevitable battles involved in entry into Canaan. He therefore commanded Moses to send representatives from each of the twelve tribes to spy out the land. The spies were to be leaders of their tribes (2,3), so that their testimonies might carry weight.

The spies' first report was realistic (25-29). They had journeyed throughout the land, seeing its people and its fruitfulness. The natural wealth of the land was evidenced by the huge cluster of grapes which then gave its name to the Valley of Eshcol. The people of Israel seem to have been disturbed by the reports of fortified cities and giant inhabitants, but Caleb soothed their worries with his words of courageous faith (30). His assurance of 'we are well able' was, however, quickly contradicted by the 'we are not able' (31) of his companions. Their report was inconsistent – giant grapes and inhabitants in a land 'that devours its inhabitants' (32)! Faith observes facts with total realism and believes that with God 'we are well able to overcome'. Unbelief twists the truth and leads to fear.

The Nephilim occur also in Genesis 6:4 and, with their enormous stature, give an almost superhuman impression. Mere mortal Israelites were indeed insignificant in comparison, so the question of 11:23 struck home with a new relevance. Is this why Israel's future leader was then given the name 'Joshua' (Saviour) (16)?

Verse 29 lists the tribes inhabiting the promised land. The Amalekites were a nomadic tribe from the southern desert regions. They dwelt in the land before the Jews entered the arena (24:20) and remained a thorn in Israel's flesh until their final destruction in the days of Hezekiah (1 Chron. 4:42,43). Until fairly recent years nothing was known of the Hittites. Some critics used to dismiss them as a fantasy of biblical writers. Now it is known that they controlled a great empire in the whole area of the Middle East from about 1800 BC until they began to decline around 1200 BC. The Jebusites gained fame from their central city, Jerusalem. The Amorites were also a great power whose national life has become well known through the famous Hammurabi and the great library of tablets found at Mari.

The travels of the spies

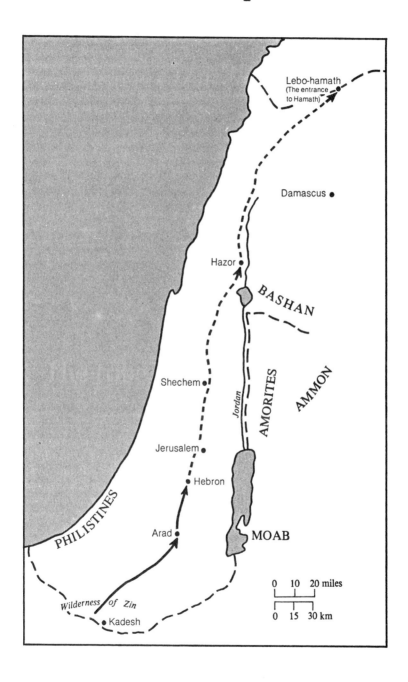

Lebo-hamath
(The entrance
to Hamath)

Damascus

Hazor

BASHAN

Shechem

Jordan

AMORITES

AMMON

Jerusalem

Hebron

MOAB

PHILISTINES

Arad

Wilderness of Zin

Kadesh

0	10	20 miles
0	15	30 km

14 The great refusal

Miracle upon miracle had proved the reality of God's power and holiness. The continual presence of the cloud was an abiding reminder that God was in the midst of his people. Despite all these evident signs (11) Israel repeatedly rebelled against the Lord and his anointed leaders (22). Many today affirm that miracles produce living faith. However, the Gospels and the Acts of the Apostles give further evidence that miracles may easily be rejected or forgotten by the hard-hearted. Israel still lacked the faith to believe that God would deliver the Canaanites into their hands and that he would keep his promises to their forefathers. Possession of the land of Canaan was promised to Israel. Knowing therefore that 'the Lord is with us' (9) they had no need to fear. Note the repetition of the word 'fear' and in contrast the repetition of 'the Lord'.

Israel's discontented rebellion again revealed itself in three ways. They murmured against the leadership of Moses and Aaron (2), adopted suicidal tendencies in which death was an escapist soft option and desired to return to the slavery of Egypt (3). The depressed or backsliding Christian may be tempted in parallel fashion.

God reacts angrily to such continual unbelief. He is not an impassionate 'cool' God (to use the expression of the Japanese theologian Koyama): he is 'hot' in anger and in love. He threatened to destroy Israel and make a new nation from Moses' descendants (12). Israel feared that her children would die in the wilderness (3) and God judged them accordingly (28-35). The first to suffer God's wrath were the faithless spies. They 'died by plague before the Lord' (37). We note that Aaron had learned his lesson and was now on Moses' side (2,5); likewise the two faithful spies, Caleb and Joshua (6).

Moses resisted the temptation to covet glory for himself and his family. He therefore prayed against the destruction of Israel and the formation of a new chosen people descended from himself. The heart of his prayer was a passionate desire for the glory of God's name and reputation. The annihilation of Israel would cause God's name to be slandered (13-16). He observed that God's greatness (17) manifested itself supremely in steadfast love and patient forgiveness (18) together with a just punishing of sin. This combination of divine justice and grace would lead to the climax of salvation history – 'all the earth shall be filled with the glory of the Lord' (21, compare Isa. 11:9; Hab. 2:14). This is the chief motive of Christian mission and should be the central ambition of every Christian.

Questions for further study and discussion on Numbers 7–14

1. 'Dialogue with God should inevitably result in more hearing than speaking' (see note on Num. 7). How can we recognise God's voice and listen to him?

2. What significance is attached to God speaking from above the mercy seat upon the ark of the testimony and from between the cherubim (7:89)?

3. In God's love there is neither Jew nor Gentile (see notes on chs. 9 and 15. Also see Gal. 3:27-29). What forms of divisive prejudice inside and outside the church are there today? What practical steps can the church as a body, and you as individuals, do to oppose this?

4. The people of Israel were guided by the cloud. How can we know that God is 'moving us on' (note on Num. 9)?

5. What caused Moses' depression and doubt? What did he do about it? How did God answer him (Num. 11)? How can Moses' experience challenge and encourage us today?

6. Use a concordance and trace what promises of God are attached to the condition of meekness (12:3).

7. In what ways does Joshua prefigure the greater Saviour, Jesus Christ (13:16)?

8. Note again the characteristics of Israel's rebellions and of Moses' reactions. What can Christians learn from these?

15 Ritual additions and clarifications

'Throughout your generations' resounds as the chapter's theme song (14,21,23,38). Forgetfulness of God's gracious saving works and the resultant rebellion had been common enough in the rugged days of the wilderness wanderings. When Israel came 'into the land' (2) and settled into a prosperous routine in this land of milk and honey, then the temptations would multiply. The people needed to start their national life with the reminder that God's commandments are not temporary.

The wearing of fringed tassels (37-41) has helped Jews to remember God's commandments throughout their history. Tradition asserts that there are eight threads and five knots in each tassel. The Hebrew for 'fringe' has a numerical value of 600 and thus the total is 613, the traditional number of commandments in the Law. Whatever our view of this typically rabbinic interpretation, the fact remains that the tassels warn their wearers against following their own desires, lest in so doing they forsake their Lord.

As stated in the corresponding chapters in Leviticus, sacrificial offerings were instituted to gain forgiveness for those who sinned unwittingly. But high handed and purposeful breaking of God's Law could only mean judgement because the person 'has despised the word of the Lord' (31). An example of such purposeful ignoring of God's commandments is immediately added (32-36). The actual sin may not seem to deserve capital punishment, but it is clear from the context that behind the sin lay rejection of God's Law. Sin and therefore also atonement were not only for individuals, but involved the whole congregation (e.g. 26).

Once again we note that the sojourner who joined himself to Israel should not be treated in any way differently from the native Israelite. The Law applied equally to the Israelite and to the stranger in Israel's midst (16). This provision should have prepared Israel for the New Testament emphasis that the middle wall of partition has been broken down through the atoning death of Christ. Jew and Gentile are one. Both sin, both need salvation, both may be justified through faith in the crucified and risen Saviour.

In days of settled prosperity materialism could turn Israel from her God. He therefore ordained that all first fruits be offered to the Lord (17-21). All we have stems from God and belongs to him. We are merely stewards of his good gifts.

16 The rebellion of Korah

Would Israel never learn her lesson? Aaron had placed himself firmly alongside Moses (3,18, etc.), but some Levites (1) and other leaders of the people (2) started yet another rebellion against Moses and the Lord. Their complaints remained the same – jealousy of Moses' leadership (3) and Aaron's priestly calling (10), discontent with God's provision in the present and an unrealistic glorification of the past (13,14).

The accusation against Moses and Aaron (3) was totally unjust (compare 11:29). It was God who had called Moses and Aaron to their high positions; they had not exalted themselves. And Moses continued to exemplify meekness. He did not answer with defensive self-righteousness, but expected the Lord to vindicate – compare the French proverb, *Qui s'excuse, s'accuse*. Moses did, however, align himself in defence of Aaron (8-11). Korah and the other sons of Levi failed to rejoice in the immense privileges accorded to them; cancer-like jealousy and bitterness had eaten into them. This so blinded their eyes that they could confidently present offerings to the Lord in expectation of his vindication of their complaints (15-18).

God's judgement was dramatic. Korah and the other principal figures in the rebellion were swallowed up by a sudden chasm in the ground. The 250 leaders of the congregation who supported them were burned to death by the divine fire which descended on their offerings. And the next day a plague consumed 14,700 of the people of Israel for, amazingly, Israel had still not learned her lesson (41-50).

The plague of God's burning wrath would have consumed the whole congregation but for the atoning ministry of Aaron. What a picture of our ministry of intercessory prayer and what a witness to the saving work of Christ – 'he stood between the dead and the living' (48). Moses knew when to reflect the holy anger of God (15) and when to send Aaron to atone for Israel's sin (46). His intercessory prayer took its stand upon the justice of God (22). He feared lest the innocent die with the guilty (26). Holiness, justice, meekness and forgiving patience form a beautiful cluster of virtues which remind us of the perfection of Jesus.

FOR MEDITATION: Moses' attitude as a model for our praying.

17 The sign of Aaron's rod

Rejection of rituals with unbiblical significance has led many of us to the opposite extreme. The insistence on the word of God without visible signs is equally unbiblical. In ch. 16 the censers of Korah and his friends were hammered into a bronze covering for the altar in order to be a perpetual sign. This sign was an unspoken sermon to remind Israel of the folly of rebellion (16:38,40). Now in ch. 17 God gives Israel a further sign to prevent complaints and murmurings (10).

Aaron's rod had already been used as a sign of God's power and authority (Exod. 7). Now it demonstrated his delegated authority to Aaron. To Jeremiah (1:11) the rod became the sign of God's promise that his word is effective. What did his rod mean to Moses when he used it to bring water from the rock (20:11)?

The Hebrew for 'rod' (*matteh*) also means 'tribe'. As the dead stick came alive and blossomed, so also there is new life for those who are God's chosen. The saving significance of new life related also to the use of *matteh* as a shepherd's staff. The gracious work of the great Shepherd is new life for those who are dead in sin.

Murmuring was the chronic sin of Israel. Such complaint against God is deadly (10-13), for it implies discontented covetousness despite all God's outpoured mercies. Could Israel not trust that all things do work together for good to those who are his elect (Rom. 8:28)? His will is perfect (Rom. 12:2) even in the wilderness. Constant grumbling reflected spiritual failure and Israel was right to repent – 'we perish, we are undone, we are all undone' (12). By grace, however, there was a negative answer to the final question of this chapter – 'are we all to perish?' No! The next chapter speaks again of the mediating priestly ministry of the priesthood.

'Rebels' (10) means literally 'sons of rebellion', a devastating substitute for the more normal term 'sons of Israel'. Ezekiel likewise frequently replaces the usual 'house of Israel' with the tragic 'house of rebellion'. Although the purpose of Aaron's rod was to stop further murmuring (5), it evidently failed. In verse 5 'make to cease' is the root used of Noah's flood abating (Gen. 8:1). The flood never recurred, but Israel's sin persisted.

CHALLENGE: Constant grumbling reflects spiritual failure.

18 Priests' and Levites' responsibilities and rewards

The priestly ministry (1-7). The answer to the question of 17:13 lay in the function of the priestly house of Aaron – 'you shall bear iniquity' (1). The Law made it abundantly clear that everyone who approached the sanctuary would die (e.g. 17:13), but the priests 'bear iniquity in connection with the sanctuary'. As priests they represented the whole people in their atoning ministry. Thus there would be 'wrath no more upon the people of Israel' (5). Even a casual reading of the Pentateuch will confirm the reality of God's holy wrath. Some critics may deny it as an inadequate understanding of the nature of God, but the atoning work of the priests was directly aimed at propitiation.

A further element in the calling of the priests was service – 'you shall serve' (7). This adds to the parallel between Jesus and the priests. He bore our iniquity and by his redemptive work fulfilled a ministry of propitiation (Rom. 3:25 – a better translation than 'expiation'). He came not to be ministered unto but to minister (Mark 10:45).

The priestly rewards (8-20). The labourer is worthy of his hire. The priests lived off the offerings of the people. They enjoyed the first-fruits (12-19) of the land, the very best of God's good gifts to Israel. The priests had no permanent inheritance like the other tribes, but they lived off what belonged to the Lord. So it could be said, 'I am your portion and your inheritance' (20). With Israel's offerings and the Levites' tithes (26-28) an ample sufficiency was guaranteed to the priests.

The Levites' inheritance (21-24). Like the priests, the Levites also had no fixed inheritance, but depended upon the tithes of the people. This was considered a direct reward for their service (21). Thus no one in Israel was independent of others. The people needed the service of the Levites and priests; they in their turn needed the tithes of the people.

The Levites' tithe for the priests (25-32). Israel's tithe offering to the Lord for the support of the Levites was now tithed again for the benefit of the priests – 'a tithe of the tithe' (26).

Some of the offerings could be eaten anywhere (31), but in other cases solemnity and sacredness pervaded them and the offering could only be eaten 'in a most holy place' (10).

19 The ashes of a heifer

Are we tempted to be bored by yet another chapter with ritual laws? Imagine the effect on the original recipients of these ordinances. Repeated and detailed statutes must have left Israel in no doubt as to the importance for God of his holiness and their need of atonement. They could hardly still question whether accidental ritual uncleanness was of fundamental importance. Careful regulations were given again and again so that they could be cleansed from 'impurity' caused by defiling contact with a dead body. Ashes from the burnt sacrifice mixed with cleansing water were sprinkled on the unclean person.

But the need for constant repetition both of the commandments and of their enactment must have left the Israelites with the feeling that the offerings were inadequate. All the shed blood of animals, the use of cedarwood, hyssop and scarlet stuff (6), the water for impurity – it all failed to conquer the problem of man's sin and uncleanness in relationship to the holiness of God. The book of Hebrews takes up this theme and extols the 'how much more' of Jesus Christ. He is the complete and final answer to man's need of cleansing from all sin, guilt and impurity.

The red heifer was totally burned with no left-overs for the priests or Levites. It was to be 'without defect', having no blemish, and it must never have been used agriculturally (2). Some have suggested that the heifer was to be red as a symbol of purifying fire, but this is not Hebrew symbolism. More probable is the idea that red represented blood, the means of atonement.

The red heifer was so particularly holy that the sacrificing priest required ritual cleansing after performing his duties (7,8). Likewise only a clean man (9) could gather up the ashes and carry them to a clean place outside the camp. The man who carried out this duty also became unclean through contact with the holy heifer (10). We cannot but be impressed by the stress on holiness. And if such holiness was attached to a heifer, how awesome must be the purity and holiness of God himself! We can only prostrate ourselves before him in worship and rejoice in the covering of Christ's righteousness which enables us to meet with him.

20 The end of an era

Moses strikes the rock (1-13). Once again hardships provoked the wrong reaction. Lack of water caused Israel to assume imminent death and therefore the people recalled rosy but unrealistic visions of comfort and plenty in Egypt. Moses and Aaron apparently obeyed the Lord's command to 'bring water out of the rock' (8). Did their sin consist of a failure to glorify the Lord: 'Shall *we* bring forth water?' (10) – a failure to 'sanctify me' (12)? Or did they manifest a contentious spirit in reaction to Israel's repeated rebellion and thus display a failure to believe in the God of patient mercy? 'You did not believe in me' (12). Deuteronomy 3:26 and Psalm 106:32 infer that Moses and Aaron suffered because of Israel's sin, but Psalm 106:33 still accuses Moses of rash words resulting from a bitter spirit.

Moses and Aaron suffered the same punishment as the rest of the generation which came out of Egypt and rebelled. They were not allowed to enter the promised land. This chapter sees the beginning of the end of the wilderness wanderings. Miriam died first (1) and then Aaron (28). The death of Moses will only be recorded at the end of his writings (Deut. 34).

Brothers begin to quarrel (14-21). Because of their common ancestry Israel assumed that Edom would be friendly. Moses' message to Edom began with the reminder that Israel was their brother (14) and he could hardly believe it when Edom refused his request. He therefore repeated his assurance that his intentions were entirely peaceful. Israel only wanted to use the recognised caravan route ('the King's Highway', 17) through Edom's territory. Edom first refused with threats of violence (18) and then backed up her repeated refusal with a show of force (20). This was the beginning of a long history of bitter battling, but at this stage Israel merely turned away and avoided a showdown.

Aaron's death (22-29). Israel's humiliating disappointment with Edom led immediately to the further tragedy of the death of Aaron 'on the border of the land of Edom' (23). Struggles in her relationship with God were to mirror Israel's battles with her neighbouring peoples.

The priestly garments of Aaron were handed on to Eleazar, his son. In themselves the garments were powerless, but they represented God's high calling and conveyed the priestly holiness they symbolised.

21 The battles begun

The Canaanites destroyed (1-3). The first battle in the campaign for Canaan was not a happy experience for Israel (1), but this distress led to a believing vow before the Lord. This promise assumed that Yahweh determined the outcome of battles. The Lord heard their prayer (3) and delivered the Canaanites into their hand. The name 'Hormah' and the word 'destroy' imply something devoted to the Lord for ritual destruction. This may suggest that the Canaanites were so unclean in God's holy judgement that they were only fit for extermination.

The bronze serpent (4-9). Israel's renewed rebellion bears as its root cause the hallmark of impatience (4). Faith was present in the previous verses, but impatience infiltrated their longing for the promised land. Sin resulted in the judgement of death through God-sent serpents (6). In their agony Israel turned in repentance which found its expression in prayer (7). The Lord answered by providing a way of salvation through the bronze serpent (8) which became effective as soon as a man looked in faith (9). Sin-judgement-repentance-prayer-salvation through faith; it is no wonder that John's Gospel quotes this passage to illustrate the gift of salvation in the death of Jesus Christ (John 3:14,15).

How pathetic that God's gracious means of salvation should be made into an idol (2 Kings 18:4) and so need to be destroyed. Is the cross facing the same danger of becoming itself the recipient of worship or prayer?

The journey continued (10-20). Having avoided the territory of Edom, Israel again turned north up the east side of the Dead Sea, thus encountering the Moabites and Amorites. The 'Book of the Wars of the Lord' (14) has evidently largely been lost, as has also the Book of Jashar (Josh. 10:12,13). Israel, like other nations of that time, kept written records of her journeyings and military triumphs. Verses 17 and 18 seem to be a working song equivalent to the Volga Boatsong, to encourage the labourers as they dug a well.

Sihon and Og defeated (21-35). Israel again sought peaceful passage (22), but was compelled to do battle (23). Defeat of Sihon led to the capture of his land and cities, so Israel took possession of her first portion of the promised land. Then God also gave victory over Og, king of Bashan, leading to further seizure of land (35). Bit by bit God gave the promised inheritance.

22 Balak and Balaam

Israel had now gained a reputation for military might (4-6) and was ready for battle with the princes of Moab. Unsure of victory through mere force of arms, Balak sought to enlist the spiritual power of Balaam (6).

Watson in the *Expositors Bible Commentary* has 'no doubt' concerning the location of Pethor on the west bank of the Euphrates in Aram near the Hittite capital city of Carchemish. Gray and Snaith in their Commentaries, however, see the possibility of 'the land of Amaw' (5) being the territory of the Ammonites. In either case it seems doubtful whether Balaam was an Israelite although he evidently served Yahweh, and his word of blessing or cursing was powerful.

Balak attempted to win the services of Balaam through the flattery of sending 'honourable' messengers (7,8,15) — it is hard to resist the blandishments of top men, especially when there are several of them (15). This high level deputation was backed up by generous offers of silver and gold (18) and the enticement of 'great honour' (17).

At first Balaam resolutely resisted temptation (13), but then his apparently firm obedience to the Lord's commands (18) wavered. He allowed the Moabites to stay with him for the night while he prayed for further guidance (19). He already knew the will of the Lord and therefore needed no further word from God. Was he hoping for different guidance because of insidious lust for Balak's riches? If so, he got what he was looking for and God commanded him to go with the Moabites (20). But this was not really God's will and his 'anger was kindled because he went' (22).

The miraculous speech and spiritual vision of the ass have been the subject of some scepticism, but to the believer all of God's creation is subject to his sovereign, miracle-working power. Through the ass Balaam escaped the drawn sword of the angel and finally his eyes were opened to God's ways and his own sin (34). He suggested to God that he should retrace his steps (34), but it was too late to turn back. He had to continue on his present course, but with renewed obedience to God's word (35,38).

THOUGHT: To the believer all of God's creation is subject to his sovereign, miracle-working power.

23 Balaam blesses Israel

The offerings of oxen and sheep (22:40) and bulls and rams (1,4,14,29) failed to follow God's carefully ordained sacrificial ritual. Nor were Balak and Balaam Levitical priests. Balak seems to have thought that the location of the sacrifices would alter what God said through Balaam (13,27), but God does not so easily repent of his unchanging word (19). God had determined where sacrifices were to be offered: neither Bamoth-baal (22:41) nor any place chosen by Balak was likely to please Yahweh! Balaam's superstitious looking for omens (24:1) also contrasted sadly with his excellent words (19).

Balaam rightly emphasised the unchanging efficacy of God's word. Neither he nor any other man had the power to alter it (8,20), for man's word is only powerful if it is in fact God's word. 'Enchantment' and 'divination' were powerless against Yahweh (23). God cannot be manipulated.

Balaam's description of God's blessing of Israel confounded Balak. Balaam saw Israel dwelling in unmolested security, unique in her peaceful prosperity (9). Israel had become the uncountable multitude which God had promised to Abraham (10; Gen. 13:16). Balaam clearly saw Israel fulfilling God's word to Abraham (24:9; compare Gen. 12:3). In Balaam's second oracle he saw Israel to be free of misfortune and trouble as she shouted with the jubilation of victory; this was based on the royal presence of the Lord their God with them (21). God's presence with Israel was founded on the saving experience of the Exodus from Egypt (22) and even the heathen Balak recognised Israel as a people who had come out of Egypt (22:11). God's blessing made Israel victoriously strong and powerful (22,24), so that people around said of her, 'What has God wrought!' (23).

Balak took Balaam to the top of Mount Pisgah because he wanted him to see only a part of the hosts of Israel and then curse them. God took Moses to the same place (Deut. 3:27; 34:1), but God showed him 'all the land'. God's purpose for Moses differed radically from Balak's purpose for Balaam; God desired to bless Israel, while Balak's aim was a curse.

TO THINK OVER: What parallels should there be between what Balaam saw in Israel and what others see in us?

24 Balaam's closing oracles

In these chapters Balaam is depicted as fundamentally obedient to the Lord's commands and word, but 31:16 throws a different light on his character. This is why Israel's adultery with Moab in ch. 25 follows immediately after the Balaam story in chs. 22–24. Jewish tradition later depicted him as 'Balaam the wicked' who had 'no share in the world to come'. The New Testament likewise only highlights his sins (2 Pet. 2:15; Jude 11; Rev. 2:14).

Balaam's third and fourth oracles (3-9, 15-24) differ in character from the first two (23:7-10,18-24). No longer were omens consulted; the snare of silver and gold was definitely rejected with the symbolic turning towards the wilderness (1). Now the 'Spirit of God came upon him' (2), so he could describe himself as a man whose eye was opened (3,15) and whose ear heard the words of God (4,16). The Hebrew is uncertain, but 'opened' seems the most likely translation. If we did not know the coming tragedy of sin (25:1-3 and 31:16), we might well deduce that Balaam had now become a truly repentant, Spirit-filled prophet of the Lord.

Prophecy does not spring from his lips. The beautiful picture of Israel living in well-ordered peace reminds us of the best of the Psalms (e.g. Psa. 1). In contrast to the wilderness experience, Israel is depicted as a well-watered garden by a river with an abundance of trees. Her buckets overflow with water (7). Water is a frequent biblical symbol of rich divine blessing (e.g. John 7:37-39).

In the final oracle comes a further example of prophetic utterance. The royal star and sceptre shall arise from Jacob and Israel (17). The crushing of the forehead of Moab may perhaps reflect the promise of Genesis 3:15, but its fulfilment came primarily in the destruction of the Moabites by Israel. However, the star and sceptre came to be the royal symbols of the Davidic kingdom whose crown was the Messiah himself, the great Son of David. Matthew shows 'the King of the Jews' being demonstrated to men through a star (Matt. 2:2) and the Book of Revelation calls Jesus 'the offspring of David, the bright morning star' (Rev. 22:16). Victory over Moab and other nations (17-24) foreshadowed the greater triumph of the Messiah. He destroys all his enemies while his people shall 'do valiantly' (18).

FOR MEDITATION AND WORSHIP: The victory which God assures his people.

Questions for further study and discussion on Numbers 15–24

1. What visual aids could be helpful to us as Christians (15:38,39)?

2. Numbers 17:5 describes the sin of murmuring. Discuss the causes and results of this sin. In what other ways do discontent and anger reveal themselves? What can we as Christians do to avoid this (compare Phil. 2:12-15)?

3. 'You shall serve' (18:7) – compare Jesus' teaching (e.g. Matt. 20:25-28) and think through how this applies to Christian leaders in the church and in society.

4. The people rebelled against God as a result of impatience (chapter 21). Why were they impatient? When God seems to delay, what is the purpose (compare John 11)?

5. How does chapter 21 illustrate Paul's statement that God's strength is made perfect in our weakness (2 Cor. 12:9)? In what ways have you experienced this in your own life?

6. How far are we affected today by Balak's enticements to Balaam (chapter 22)?

7. What is the harm in 'looking for omens' (24:1)?

8. How is God's holy wrath revealed in these chapters? How would you answer the comment that this is not compatible with the God of forgiving love revealed in the New Testament?

25 Sin – jealousy – wrath

Balak had failed to defeat Israel through the curses of Balaam. He knew that direct trial of strength in battle was hopeless (22:3,4,6). Lacking spiritual or military muscle, Moab and their allies, the Midianites (see 22:4.7), defeated Israel by the wiles of their girls. Israel's sexual sin led directly to idolatrous worship of the gods of Moab.

How often through the history of God's people have men been led away from the Lord through love of a beautiful but heathen girl! Today's Christian faces the same temptation.

Zimri blatantly and provocatively flaunted his sin 'in the sight of the whole congregation' (6). Moses and the spiritual leaders of Israel were already weeping in repentance for the sin of Israel, for the wrath of God was 'kindled against Israel' (3). Phinehas, Aaron's grandson, accepted the challenge and killed both Zimri and the Midianite woman. The shedding of this representative blood made atonement for Israel (13) and 'the plague was stayed' (8).

Paul in his letters to the Corinthians evidently has this chapter in his mind as he counters their sexual sin (1 Cor. 5:1-5). He refers to this chapter in warning against immorality (1 Cor. 10:8) and it is likely that his use of the concept of being 'yoked together' (2 Cor. 6:14 – RSV 'mis-mated') refers to Numbers 25:3,5.

Sexual sin with its companion idolatry is particularly abhorrent to God. His wrath burned with a deep jealousy at the rebellion of his people. Thousands perished in the resultant plague – the numerical discrepancy in 1 Corinthians 10:8 may be because Paul is making allowance for those killed by the judges (5).

God commissioned Moses with the task of avenging the wiles of the Midianites. This proved to be Moses' final campaign before his death (31:2). The jealous wrath of God demanded retribution. Israel herself and the Midianites had to be judged.

Phinehas however was rewarded for his priestly action of atonement in which he displayed the jealousy of God (11). God granted him and his descendants a covenant of peace and of a perpetual priesthood. This is finally fulfilled in Jesus, the ultimate and perfect priest, who inaugurates the new covenant of abiding peace.

26 The second census

As in chapter 1 this was again a military census (2), but with the addition of the names of clans within the tribes (compare Gen. 46 and Exod. 6). Such lists may appear boring, but this routine numbering was a necessary preparation for effective future action. Routine administration often plays a vital part in God's work. Here it enabled Moses to make plans for the advance into the promised land of Canaan; accurate statistics were also needed for the proper division of the land among the various tribes and families (52-56); and a third reason for the numbering of Israel at this stage was to check that none of the previous generation remained alive except Caleb and Joshua (64,65). Thus all was ready for the battles that lay ahead as Israel moved forward into her inheritance.

The differences between the numbers in chapter 1 and this chapter require some comment (compare note on chapter 1). Simeon had lost some two thirds of its fighting men, while Manasseh had increased by similar proportions. Manasseh and Ephraim seem to have exchanged their totals (are their names here in the wrong order?).

In listing the Reubenites the names Dathan and Abiram emerge (9), which leads to the interesting comment about the sons of Korah the Levite (11, compare chapter 16). Whereas Dathan's and Abiram's whole families were swallowed up in God's judgement, the sons of Korah survived and we owe to them Psalms 42-49,84,85,87,88. Judgement can give way to grace.

Behind this chapter lies the typical Old Testament assumption that large numbers of sons and descendants denote God's blessing: 'Happy is the man who has his quiver full of them' (Ps. 127:5). The people wanted large families in order to keep God's command to 'fill the earth and subdue it' and so have dominion over all creatures (Gen. 1:28). Today's massive population explosion has so filled the earth that we are in danger of losing control of the created order. Therefore the control of population growth may now demonstrate greater obedience to God's commands and purposes than the procreation of many children.

THOUGHT: Routine administration often plays a vital part in God's work.

27 Two problems of continuity

Zelophehad's inheritance (1-11). Although it had not been specifically laid down, rights of inheritance were assumed to pass through the male descendants. In chapter 26 it was only the sons who were numbered and this seems to have applied to rights of inheritance as well as to military responsibility. The five daughters of Zelophehad raised the question of their father who died without sons. With characteristic wisdom Moses did not immediately judge the case with the inflexibility of former traditions (compare Lev. 24:12; Num. 9:8; 15:34), but 'brought their case before the Lord' (5). God gave a new application to the existing law – God never changes his law, but frequently requires a new application. The rights of women are furthered in this statute.

Moses' successor (12-23). Moses must have been deeply disappointed not to have been permitted to lead Israel into the promised land. But he did not wallow in his own feelings. His concern was for the future leadership and welfare of Israel (16,17). He knew the people's need of a leader, lest they become a scattered flock, each going his own way (compare the refrain in Judges after Joshua's death, 'Israel did what was evil', 'every man did what was right in his own eyes' because 'there was no king in Israel'). Ezekiel reflects the same thought (ch. 34), as does Jesus (Matt. 9:36-38). God's purpose for his people was that they might be a united 'congregation' (14,16,17,19,20,21,22): the Hebrew *edah* means to come together and thus also to agree (compare Amos 3:3). God desired his people to join together in agreement and so march forward into battle as a united force.

Moses' successor was to be Joshua, 'a man in whom is the spirit' (18). Deuteronomy 34:9 states that through the imposition of Moses' hands Joshua was 'full of the spirit of wisdom'. The laying on of hands was a common sign by which the blessing or authority of the Lord was passed on to another person (e.g. Gen. 48:14; Matt. 9:18; 19:13; Acts 6:6; 13:3). Moses invested Joshua with 'some of his authority', but not the privilege of unmediated knowledge of God's will (21). As Kidner says, 'Henceforth the functions of leader and mediator of revelation would remain distinct until they were united again in Christ.'

TO THINK OVER. What is the role of leadership as seen in this chapter? What qualities are demanded? How, if at all, do the ideas of leadership in our churches differ?

28–29 The calendar of offerings

Covering much the same ground as Leviticus 23, these chapters detail the daily (3-8), weekly (9,10) and monthly (11-15) offerings and the annual pageant of special festivities, starting with the first month and the Passover (16) and climaxing with the seventh month's succession of celebrations (29:1-38). John calls the final day of the seventh month 'the great day' (John 7:37).

The normal offerings of the day were never replaced by the greater offerings of the special occasions. The regular sacrifices continued; the extra festivals were always in addition – note the repeated 'besides' (28:10,15,24,31, etc.). Regular daily practices should never be edged out by red-letter festivities.

As the seventh day and the seventh year had particular significance in Jewish life, so also the seventh month marked the highlight of the annual calendar. The holiday was celebrated with the blowing of trumpets (29:1) on the first day. The tenth day contained the great Day of Atonement (29:7-11; compare Lev. 16) and then on the fifteenth day there began the remarkable eight days of the Feast of Tabernacles (29:12-38). The course of those eight days was marked by the daily reduction of the required number of bulls for sacrifice. Beginning with thirteen the number went down one each day and then on the eighth day it was suddenly reduced from seven to a mere one. Does this look forward by implication to the yet greater climax when the sacrifice of bulls would be needed no more?

We notice once more that the primary purpose of the offerings was to satisfy and please the Lord rather than merely to atone for the sins of the people – note the emphasis on 'my' and 'me' in 28:2. The manward element was always present, but essentially the offerings were 'a pleasing odour to the Lord'. True biblical religion must always be God-centred – 'Let the world determine the agenda', the old slogan of the 1968 WCC Uppsala Conference, typifies an unbiblical man-centredness.

The form of work prohibited on the Passover (28:18) and other special feasts (28:26; 29:1, etc.) was 'servile' (AV) rather than 'laborious' (RSV). This perhaps reflected Israel's joyous freedom from the slavery of sin. It is noteworthy that the usual commandment to do no work on the Sabbath is absent here (28:9,10).

THOUGHT: True religion must always be God-centred.

30 Responsibility for vows

This chapter must be seen in the context of other passages which give more general teaching concerning vows (e.g. Lev. 27; Deut. 23:21-23). Here we are given specific statutes for a girl 'in her youth, within her father's house' (3-5), for a wife (6-8) and for a widow or divorced woman (9-15).

It is here assumed that women were subject to the authority of their husbands or fathers who had the responsibility to negate or affirm the woman's vow if they knew of it. Silence assumed agreement. The Hebrew woman was never free and independent. While young and unmarried she was under her father; when married her husband 'rules over her' (Gen. 3:16). This pattern of male authority continues into the New Testament where children are to be obedient to their parents (Eph. 6:1) and wives are to be subject to their husbands (Eph. 5:22). Paul, however, underlines the reverse side of this coin – male responsibility. The father is not to provoke his children to anger (Eph. 6:4) and the husband is to love his wife 'as Christ loved the church and gave himself up for her' (Eph. 5:25). Love serves (Gal. 5:13), gives (John 3:16) and causes us to count others better than ourselves (Phil. 2:3). When the woman's obedience is matched by such love from her husband, the formula for harmony is complete.

In the New Testament the practice of making vows continues. God himself 'swore by himself' (Heb. 6:13), an angel swore 'by him who lives for ever' (Rev. 10:6) and to reinforce his words Paul also 'calls God to witness against' him (2 Cor. 1:23). This must be balanced against the apparent total prohibition of vows by Jesus (Matt. 5:33-37) and also by James (James 5:12). The practice of vowing had been grossly misused (Mark 7:10-13) and led to hair-splitting debates which denigrated God's truth (Matt. 23:16-22). Therefore Jesus emphasises the simple requirement of a disciple that his word alone should be trustworthy. If a man's word cannot be trusted, the basis of life in society is undermined. In fact God's purpose in giving these statutes is not merely to ensure right behaviour in the individual, but to further right relationships 'between a man and his wife, and between a father and his daughter' (16).

CHALLENGE: Jesus emphasises the simple requirement of a disciple that his word alone should be trustworthy.

31 Vengeance against Midian

Biblical vengeance is no personal vendetta of spite and bitterness, but God's holiness active in just retribution for sin. In the Bible men do not have the right to vengeance; this is God's prerogative. If men take to themselves God's unique right, then God will avenge himself on them (e.g. Ezek. 25:12-17). Vengeance belongs to the Lord (Deut. 32:35; Psa. 94:1; Rom. 12:19; Heb. 10:30) and a brief glance at a concordance reveals the biblical emphasis on 'the Lord's vengeance' and his 'day of vengeance'.

Moses and Israel were, however, called to be God's instruments in executing 'the Lord's vengeance' (3). The Midianites were judged for their evil ensnaring of God's people and Balaam shared their fate (8) for he had led them into their sin by his bad counsel (16). The contaminating influence of this corrupt people was to be totally eradicated by the slaughter of every male (7) and every woman who could be the means of bearing further Midianite children (17). Other women, cattle and booty could be kept as spoil for the people of Israel. This booty was divided equally between the men who had fought in the battle and the rest of the congregation (27). A small offering from this booty was dedicated to the Lord. The much smaller portion from the warriors was given to Eleazar, the priest (28,29), while the larger share from the rest of the congregation came to the Levites (30).

It seems that private looting had taken place (53), which could have brought Israel into sin and judgement (compare Josh. 7:1), for the corruption of Midian made all their possessions unclean. All contact with them required ritual cleansing (24), while the booty itself also needed to be purified by fire or water (21-23) – note the repetition of 'purify' and 'clean' (19-24). It was therefore brought to the Lord by the army leaders (48-54), thus 'making atonement' (50). Atonement is not only through ritual sacrifice, but also includes a repentance that reverses sinful practices.

The gold from the army leaders was placed in the tent of meeting as a 'memorial' (54), so that the people of Israel should never again forget their call to what C.H.M. in his commentary calls 'rigid separation'.

THOUGHT: Atonement is not only through ritual sacrifice, but also includes repentance that reverses sinful practices.

32 'Do not take us across the Jordan'

Reuben's and Gad's proposition (1-5). Circumstances pointed to an inheritance for these two tribes east of Jordan, although God had promised Israel the possession of the land of Canaan. They had 'a very great multitude of cattle' and they noted that Jazer and Gilead were suited to cattle rearing (1). Such material circumstances may appear inadequate grounds for altering the revealed purposes of God, but at least the two tribes had the grace to put their proposition to Moses, Eleazar and the leaders of the congregation (2). They did not act in rebellious independence.

Moses' answer (6-15). Moses feared that any weakening of the people's solidarity could cause the remaining tribes to waver in their intention to conquer Canaan. Israel had been discouraged by the spies' report (9) and Moses was apprehensive lest they lose heart again. The thought of a further period of judgement in the wilderness (15) made his words to the two tribes exceedingly strong (14). He knew how easily Israel could be discouraged – note the twofold 'discouraged' (7,9). The sons of Reuben and Gad had no right to desert the armies of Israel at the start of the campaign. Their strong emphasis on 'cattle' (1,4) was no excuse!

A satisfactory solution (16-42). The sons of Reuben and Gad found a wise compromise solution. How much better than a hard-hearted quarrel! Their armed men would fight alongside those of the other tribes until Canaan was conquered. Then they would return to possess their desired territory east of Jordan. Meanwhile they would leave their wives, children and flocks in the fortified cities of Gilead (26). This dangerous step of faith was rewarded with success (compare Josh. 22). Their chosen inheritance became their 'possession before the Lord' (22), not a token of disobedience. In taking over the cities of the Amorites and building further on their foundations, they changed the Baal-orientated names (38). In Scripture a new name always signifies a new character. Syncretistic compromise with heathen deities was to be shunned.

An agreed solution was one thing; fulfilment of the promise was still required. Moses therefore prefaced his words with 'If you will do this' (20,29) and reminded them to do what they had promised (24). If their words led to action, all would be well; if not, then they had 'sinned against the Lord' and they could be sure their sin would find them out (23). God is just – both righteousness and sin have their inevitable consequences.

33:1-49 The log of the journey

Forty stages are listed for the forty years of wilderness wanderings – eleven stages from Rameses in Egypt to the wilderness of Sinai, twenty-one stages to Ezion-geber and on to Kadesh in the wilderness of Zin, nine final stages to the plains of Moab. It seems clear that the list is not complete: for example, there must have been a camping place between Ezion-geber and Kadesh which are many miles apart (fifty miles according to Snaith and seventy miles according to Kidner – this depends on the exact siting of the two places).

Comment on the list of encampments is minimal. It is all the more striking, therefore, to observe the only two before Kadesh (9,14). Both are concerned with water and we can picture the arid hardships of forty years' wandering in the wilderness. Yet the testimony of Moses is of a bountiful God who had met every need throughout those years in every circumstance (Deut. 2:7).

The only other comments included in the list of encampments are the major event of the death of Aaron (38,39), followed by the commencement of battle for the possession of the land (40, compare 20:22–21:3).

'Triumphantly' (3) may equally be translated 'defiantly' (Exod. 14:8). The word signifies height and can thus indicate high-handed self-exaltation (e.g. 15:30).

Verse 2 highlights the critical debate whether Moses wrote part or all of the Pentateuch. E. J. Young in his *Introduction to the Old Testament* quotes this verse as 'a strong argument for the Mosaic authorship of the entire Pentateuchal narrative'. This perhaps overstates the case, for some passages clearly issue from an editorial pen (e.g. Deut. 34), though the main body of these books probably does stem from Moses' authorship.

Verse 2 demonstrates the pattern of biblical inspiration. The Lord commands, and Moses writes. This is no mere human composition apart from the directing word of the Lord; likewise it denies a purely divine authorship without human participation. This is important not only for our own right understanding of Scripture, but also for our discussions with Muslims. Arabic has two words for 'reveal'. *Wahy* is the perfect Word of God mediated to man by an angel without human co-operation (e.g. the Qur'ān), while *Ilham* passes through conscious human means and is therefore fallible. The Christian doctrine of Scripture is neither *Wahy* nor *Ilham* – God speaks perfectly through man.

33:50–34:29 Careful planning

Well-defined goals. Although today we are still unsure of the exact location of some of the place names, the broad outline of Israel's proposed borders is clear (see any Bible atlas). The people knew exactly the extent of the coming campaign. They also knew God's purposes for them in relationship to the conquered Canaanite peoples. There was to be no compromising intermingling with heathen remnants. They should 'drive out all the inhabitants of the land' (52) and destroy everything connected with the morally perverted and idolatrous religion of Canaan. Any failure to cleanse the land of contaminating elements could only result in continuous temptation and trouble (55). As a result of such failure God would drive Israel out of the land just as he desired to remove the Canaanites (56). Future history showed the absolute accuracy of God's words through Moses.

Clear lines of authority. God never abdicates his ultimate authority. The lot remained the final arbiter of who gained the various portions of the land (54). But under God leadership was delegated to chosen men for the task of dividing the land (16-29). Carefully designated leadership structures are vital for the on-going life of God's people. We note that the highest echelon of leadership was according to personal quality (Eleazar and Joshua), while the next stage of authority was according to the natural structures of society, one man from each tribe. Of these men only Caleb is mentioned elsewhere in Scripture.

A just society. The use of the lot might appear to promote inequitable division of the land, but actually the lot was surely used only for the choice between almost equal portions of land. Each tribe inherited according to its size (54). Unfair inequality may be a source of bitterness, jealousy and division even amongst the people of God. In the Old Testament justice in Israel included a fundamental equality as the base on which each family could build its fortunes. In the New Testament church justice is demonstrated by an unselfish love which delights to give and to share.

THOUGHT: Carefully delegated leadership structures are vital for the on-going life of God's people.

35 Special cities

Cities for Levites (1-8). While other tribes were given whole areas of land as their inheritance, the Levites were not to have such a settled existence (18:23). They shared the insecurity of the unfortunate (Deut. 14:29). Nevertheless they did need somewhere to live and God designated forty-eight cities with their surrounding pasture lands. The Mishnah recognises the apparent contradiction in the extent of the pasture land (4,5). One solution it suggests is that 'the one thousand cubits are the outskirts (which pertain to the city but may not be built upon) while the two thousand cubits are the Sabbath limit'. Another Rabbi agrees that the thousand cubits are the outskirts, but believes 'the two thousand cubits are the surrounding fields and vineyards' (Sotah 5:3).

Cities of refuge (9-34). Included in the number of the Levites' cities were the six cities of refuge, three each side of the Jordan (14). The provision of these cities ensured a fair trial for all involved in murder or manslaughter. The clear distinction here made between purposeful murder and killing 'without intent' (11,15) might easily be overlooked and ignored by 'the avenger of blood' (19,21, etc.). Despite the fact that vengeance 'belongs to the Lord' (see ch.31), the practice of blood vengeance evidently continued and realism demanded a refuge for the accidental killer. A fair trial also required more than one witness, lest prejudice or bribery corrupt the course of justice. Although it was the responsibility of the whole congregation to judge (24,25), executions were performed by the 'avenger of blood' himself.

The basis and the purpose of justice was the holiness of Yahweh. He dwelt in the land 'in the midst of the people of Israel' (34). Defilement of this land therefore offended the absolute holiness of God. The shedding of blood polluted (33), so murder could only be expiated by the blood of the guilty party. He could never be freed through the payment of a ransom – rich and poor alike had to pay the ultimate price. Even the man guilty of accidental manslaughter was restricted to the cities of refuge until the high priest died; with blood on his hands he could not wander through the land lest it be polluted (32,33). If he foolishly strayed outside the limits of the city of refuge, he was liable to death at the hands of the avenger (26-28).

36 A problem of inheritance

The apparently just decision of chapter 27 with regard to the inheritance of the daughters of Zelophehad now presented a problem. It seemed to negate the carefully designated equality between the tribes. If the ladies married outside their own tribe of Manasseh, their inheritance would be added to the tribe of their husband and would not revert to the sons of Manasseh at the Jubilee; it would then become the permanent inheritance of the other tribe and thus overturn the whole aim of the Jubilee.

Once again we find Moses giving judgement in this case 'according to the word of the Lord' (5). His decision limited the heiresses to marriage within their own tribe (8) – a limitation they happily accepted (10-12). In a society where arranged marriages formed the normal pattern, Moses' judgement would not have seemed unfair and limiting as it would in freer modern societies. Nevertheless, it demonstrates the principle that privilege and possessions sometimes bring with them cramping responsibilities. The willing obedience of these five ladies forms a happy conclusion to the story of Israel in Numbers, a story which has so often been marred by failure, disobedience and sin.

Questions for further study and discussion on Numbers 25–36

1. Why is it that Paul forbids marriage between Christians and non-Christians (see note on Num. 25, and compare 2 Cor. 6:14)?

2. We pray for the spiritual leaders of the church, but how often do we pray for those involved in the routine administration (see note on Num. 26)? What routine jobs are there in a church? What difficulties are there for the people who do them?

3. If a husband asks his wife to do something that is wrong or unreasonable, is it biblical that she should obey him (Num. 30)?

4. How far is equality of possessions or opportunity required among the people of God (Acts 4:32)?

5. What attitude should we take to injustice and lack of 'fellowship' in non-Christian society?

6. What 'well defined goals' should the Christian church have (compare note on 33:50–34:29)?

7. What 'clear lines of authority' are suggested in the New Testament for the church?

8. What is Jesus' attitude to the inspiration of Scripture (compare 33:2)?

Analysis of Deuteronomy

1 Recalling the great refusal

The introductory comments to Moses' speech (1-5) remind us briefly of the geographical and historical facts which form the backcloth to his words. He wished to prepare Israel for the future when he would be dead and Joshua would lead them into the promised land of Canaan. As so often, the best preparation for the future was a review of the past. These early verses highlight the victories over Sihon and Og (4); they imply the folly of Israel's rebellious sin – note the contrast between 'eleven days' journey' (2) and 'in the fortieth year' (3); and they significantly introduce the new expression 'all Israel' (1) to stress the solidarity of God's people from generation to generation and at any one given time. In Leviticus and Numbers 'the people' (lit. 'children of Israel') is the normal term, but in Deuteronomy both expressions are common (1,3).

A reminder of the task (6-8). With the assurance of a specific commandment from 'the Lord their God' and his covenanted and sworn promise to their patriarchal ancestors, Israel could surely obey – 'go in and take possession'.

Preparation for Moses' removal (9-18). It is always hard to find a successor to a dynamic one-man leadership. Moses' delegation of authority prepared the ground for Joshua to assume his mantle. Moses found himself unable to bear the burden alone because Israel had now become such a multitude (10) and because of their troublesome 'strife' (12). The encouragement of God's blessings and trustworthiness was tempered with a reminder of Israel's weakness and sin.

The cause of forty years in the wilderness (19-40). Israel's restricted, self-centred vision with its emphasis on 'we', 'us' and 'our' (27-28) contrasted markedly with Moses' God-directed faith and assurance based on 'the Lord our/your God' (19,20,21,25, etc.). The almighty God was related in a personal way to Israel; he fought for them (30), bore them like a father cradles his baby son (31) and led them in safety by day and night (33). The Israelites standing before Moses to hear his words were intimately united to their rebellious fathers (compare 'all Israel') and so Moses addressed them as if it were they who had rebelled (e.g. the use of 'you' and 'your'). Moses' reminder of the faithfulness of Caleb and Joshua opened the door for their acceptance as the new leaders.

2 The wanderings and first conquest

This chapter covers much of the same material as Numbers 20 and 21, but deals with it differently. The emphasis here is on God's commandments and Israel's obedience, although passing reference is made to the judgement of Israel's disobedient generation (14,15) However, v. 7 is more representative of this chapter than v. 15.

Parallel to Israel's fear at the report of the spies (1:28), this chapter reveals Israel as the cause of trembling to other peoples (25). But unlike Israel's fear, the nations' dread was caused by the Lord himself. This chapter's continual emphasis on the sovereign initiative and working of God (e.g. 33,36) is balanced by repeated underlining of Israel's part in obedience to God's commandments (e.g. 33,34). When Israel was obedient to the directions of her almighty God, her former fears of cities with high walls proved unnecessary (36). Faithful submission to the Lord overcomes all obstacles.

God's sovereignty relates not only to his own people of Israel, but also to the fate of the heathen nations (5,9,19,21). Although Israel was God's elect people, she was not permitted to grasp whatever land she desired. She was limited to the inheritance God had chosen for her, while he deliberately appointed other territories as the possession of other nations. It is reassuring for us today to know that the movements of nations in history are directly under the sovereign control of the Lord. To some he gives new territorial possessions, while others are ripe for judgement and destruction (e.g. the Amorites).

The apparent contradiction between v. 29 and both Numbers 20:21, and Deuteronomy 23:4 may be reconciled by the explanation of Thompson (Tyndale Commentary) that Moab refused transit through the heart of their territory, but allowed passage around the outskirts. Manley (*New Bible Commentary*) suggests that outlying areas of Moab did not follow their leaders' rejection of Israel's request.

'Caphtorim' (23) appears to be an early name for the Philistines, but it is less certain exactly where Caphtor was. As Von Rad says in his SCM Commentary, Caphtor 'is usually identified with Crete; but Cappadocia has also been suggested'. Thompson widens this to 'the sea coasts and islands of the Aegean Sea'. Outside of the Bible nothing is known of the Zamzummim (20), while the Rephaim may not be a particular race but an indeterminate collection of giant peoples.

3 The retrospect concluded

As in the previous chapter where it was *God* who gave victory through the obedient co-operation of Israel, so in this chapter it is again *God* who gave Israel the land to possess (18,20,28). But, as the servant of the Lord, Moses was also able to say 'I gave the territory' (12,16). God's plan to use mere man as his agent in the performance of his will is evidence of his tremendous grace. What a privilege to be in God's service!

Again we note how Moses' chronicle of past divine victories had the purpose of encouraging Joshua as he led Israel over the Jordan (21). Israel was prone to paralysing fear which could prevent her from moving forward into the possession of God's promises. Moses therefore warned Joshua 'You shall not fear them' (22) and reassured him of the basis for fearlessness – 'It is the Lord your God who fights for you'.

In his description of past victories Moses stressed the strength of Israel's defeated enemies. Victory over Og, King of Bashan, meant the capture of sixty fortified cities 'with high walls, gates and bars' (5). Og was evidently a giant ('Rephaim' may well mean 'giants'), as evidenced by his outsize bed. The word for 'bed' is also translated 'couch' (e.g. Amos 3:12, and 6:4 where a different word is used for 'bed'). In Aramaic this word is also used for a bier. Despite Gray's note in his International Critical Commentary to show the possibility that Og's 'bed' was perhaps a sarcophagus, Von Rad rejects this suggestion as hardly possible, but Thompson (Tyndale) and Craigie (New International Commentary) accept it.

Although Moses had already seen much of God's powerful working on behalf of his people, he longed to be allowed to enter the promised land and see the fullness of God's grace to Israel (24). He was, however, representatively involved in Israel's sin ('on your account', 26) and thus had come into a culpable error. But God allowed him to see Israel's future inheritance from the top of Pisgah and gave him responsibility for the encouragement and strengthening of Joshua, his successor (28). God's might is so incomparably great that even Moses had only begun to experience his majestic power (24). True discipleship means constant growth in knowledge and love

---

CHALLENGE: True discipleship means constant growth in knowledge and love.

4 'Lest you forget'

Israel was always liable to forget both the past mercies and the judgements of their God. Prosperity and success could increase this tendency. Moses therefore warned them to 'give heed' (1) to God's statutes, to keep his commandments and do them (2,6). They should remember the plague at Baal-peor. A careful and diligent walk with God was required if they were not to forget what they had seen and learned (9), and all that God had shown them was to be passed on from generation to generation. Fear of the Lord and obedience to his commandments were to be taught to their children (10).

Punctilious observance of God's word is the condition for entry into and enjoyment of the promised inheritance; nothing may be added to or subtracted from God's word. The Bible ends on the same note – entry into the holy city and enjoyment of the tree of life is conditional on neither adding to nor taking away from the 'words of the book' (Rev. 22:18,19).

Israel's greatest temptation in Canaan was to be the adoption of the idolatrous practices of the land. Moses therefore gave protracted and specific teaching on this subject (15-31). On the awe-inspiring occasion of the giving of the Law at Horeb the Lord spoke with audible voice from the midst of visible fire (36), but Israel 'saw no form' (15). Likewise their worship should never include the making of a graven image in any form.

Rather than imitating the idolatrous religion of other peoples, Israel should attract the admiration of the nations for her wisdom and understanding (6). Her glory would be that she 'has a God so near' to her (7) and that she possessed statutes and ordinances of unparalleled righteousness (8). Through her righteousness and her close walk with God Israel should therefore attract the nations to the Lord (compare Matt. 5:16 and Isaiah 60:3).

Idolatry was folly, for Yahweh is unique and incomparable (32-40). The events of Horeb and the Exodus from Egypt demonstrated that Yahweh is the one God. 'There is no other besides him' (35, 39). Moses was firmly monotheistic in his theology: he did not tolerate the idea of various religions and gods having equal validity (see M. Goldsmith's *Don't just stand there*, IVP).

Verse 19 (compare 2:30) seems to make God the author of evil. The sovereign God confirms man in his evil tendencies, but in grace allows freedom of choice and ultimately overrules everything for the good of his elect children (Rom. 8:28).

5 'Face to face at the mountain'

Undue chatty familiarity with God is incompatible with the awesome experience of Horeb. The voice, the fire and the holiness of God's presence engraved a deep and fearful impression of God's glory and greatness (24) upon the people of Israel. Awe at the glorious majesty of God forms a good prelude to the assured and bold entry into his presence granted to us in Christ. The Old Testament covenant and law still influence our attitude to God under the new covenant of grace in the blood of Christ.

The Ten Commandments display God's way of life for Israel, but her relationship with God was through the God-initiated covenant. The Ten Commandments express the covenant in its practical outworking (4:13). God's covenants, like enforced political treaties, seem one-sided. It is God who makes the covenant and speaks to Israel (2-4) and the commandments commence with a declaration of his lordship over Israel. This lordship, however, reveals itself in grace and salvation (6).

Struck by the terror of a face-to-face encounter with God's glory, Israel rightly (28) demanded a mediator (5,23-27). Moses 'stood between' the Lord and the people to mediate 'the word of the Lord' (5), just as the priests stood between Israel and God to mediate atonement. Both find their climax and fulfilment in Christ, who not only mediates the word and atonement to his people; he *is* the Word (John 1) and he *is* the Lamb of God, the way to the Father.

In the list of the ten 'words' we note the greater detail given to the commandments concerning idolatry and the Sabbath. As we saw in the last chapter, idolatry was Israel's greatest temptation, and therefore needed underlining. The Sabbath was the hallmark and touchstone of Israel's loyalty and obedience to the Lord (e.g. Jer. 17:21-27, Ezek. 20:10-24; Amos 8:5). Israel were reminded of their days as slaves in Egypt (15, note the difference from Exod. 20), for the Sabbath protected the weak and the foreigner in Israel's midst. It was not only for Israel's sake, therefore, but extended to Gentiles (compare 4:6). The reputation of God's name remains always of paramount importance – not only in the Sabbath commandment, but also in the whole order of the Ten Commandments.

THOUGHT: Awe at the glorious majesty of God forms a good prelude to the assured and bold entry into his presence granted to us in Christ.

6 God's perfect way

This chapter impresses us with the gloriously perfect will of God. His commandments are matched by promises of blessing (24) while Israel's strict obedience runs parallel to her love for God (5) and her enjoyment of a 'land flowing with milk and honey' (3). No wonder Psalm 119 and the best of Jewish traditions have seen God's law as a source of joy. God's words should never become an optional extra in life. Daily conversation in the home or street should centre on his law (7); it should remain ever before each man as the focus of his consciousness (8) and as the obvious authority in home life (9). In their use of the phylactery (worn on the forehead) and the *mezuzah* (attached to the door post), the Jews have taken these verses (8,9) literally. Such visible signs can serve a useful purpose, but legalism and the desire for human recognition of one's piety remain, in these and similar situations, a powerful temptation.

This idyllic picture of God's perfect way for his people shone in a dark surrounding frame of Israel's failure and sin. The high calling to love the Lord with *'all* your heart, *all* your soul and *all* your might' gave little hope that Israel would 'do all this commandment' and thus find 'righteousness' (25). The warning memories of past failures (16) were to haunt the future. Prosperity easily induced coldness of heart and forgetfulness of mind (10-12), so that idolatry again reared its ugly head and brought with it God's anger and destruction (13-15).

The combination of an awareness of God's high calling and the frustration of human weakness, failure and sin makes the Law a schoolmaster to bring us to Christ (Gal. 3:24). He is God's unique solution to the problem of man's inability to achieve the supremely high standards of God's holiness and love.

Again we note the emphasis on teaching the children (2,7,20). Traditionally the almost credal affirmation of verse 4 has become central to Jewish faith and teaching. The particularity of Yahweh as 'our' God is widened by rabbinic interpretation which teaches that the 'oneness' of God declares him to be King in all four corners of the world. This universal sovereignty of God is a basic principle for missionary involvement.

THOUGHT: Daily conversation in the home or the street should centre on God's law; it should remain before each man as the focus of his consciousness and as the obvious authority in home life.

7 'A people holy to the Lord'

In preparation for possession of Canaan, Israel needed instruction on how to deal with the nations of that land. These nations were 'greater and mightier' than Israel (1), but Yahweh was a 'great and terrible God' (21) who would clear these nations away (1,22), give them over to Israel (2) and dispossess them. Israel was not to be afraid of them (17-21).

Israel was 'holy to the Lord' (6), belonging utterly and only to their God. There could therefore be no compromise with the corrupt nations of Canaan. Intermarriage was forbidden (3), for this led almost inevitably to religious declension and so to judgement (4). 'Utterly destroy' is the key-word; there could be no agreement or covenant with corrupt peoples (2). Everything associated with their idolatrous and immoral religions was to be totally destroyed – even the silver or gold over the idols was to be burned (25).

The removal and destruction of the Canaanite nations would, however, be gradual – 'little by little' (22). This throws light on the future history shown in the book of Joshua. It also illustrates the patience of God in the spiritual development of his children – if growth is too rapid, it may lead to the 'wild beast' of pride.

No grounds for pride were allowed to Israel. Moses reminded them that they 'were the fewest of all peoples' (7). Israel was in no way greater or mightier than the other nations (1). The reason for divine election is shrouded in mystery – 'it is because the Lord loves you' (8), but there can be no explanation of why he loved them. God's repeated practice of choosing the weak, the insignificant and the youngest son makes pride a foolishness. God's glory committed to earthen vessels ensures that it is his name which is honoured and praised.

There is a marked contrast between the immoral idols of the Canaanites and the loving holiness of Yahweh. He is faithful to his word and covenant promises, demonstrating a deep and abiding steadfast love (9). His holiness and truth are further evidenced by his jealous destruction of those who hated him (10). The abundance of his loving blessings (13-15) is conditional on obedience (12).

THOUGHT: God's glory committed to earthen vessels ensures that it is his name which is honoured and praised.

8 'To do you good in the end'

What a list of God's gracious activities on behalf of his people! He led (2,15), humbled (2,3), tested (2,16), instructed (3), disciplined (5), delivered from Egypt (14), fed and gave water (15,16). God purposed to train and teach his people and this would finally be for their good (16), although Israel might grumble at the unaccustomed manna (3) – how traditional many are! – and fail to be thankful for God's continuous provision (4).

With the coming material prosperity (7-10) Israel needed to know that the word of the Lord is more important than bread (3). Jesus faced the same basic temptation to give undue prominence to 'bread' (Matt. 4:3,4). It is of God's goodness and grace that we 'eat and are full' (10). What would be Israel's response to prosperity? Would they 'bless the Lord for the good land he has given' (10) or would they 'forget the Lord by not keeping his commandments' (11)? The answer depended on whether they were humbled by their experiences in the wilderness or began to say 'my power and the might of my hand have gotten me this wealth' (17). The dangers from a multiplication of flocks, money and possessions (13) were hearts 'lifted up' and God forgotten (14). The rich blessings of the Lord could so easily be turned to dust (19,20).

Wealth is not in itself evil or necessarily corrupting. It is God who gives the 'power to get wealth' (18). He gave Israel the 'good land' (10) with its abundance of water (compare Num. 33), food and raw materials (9). It is the 'love of money' (not money itself) which is the root of all evils (1 Tim. 6:10), but humble stewardship and gratitude to the Lord turn wealth into a blessing.

The New Testament emphasis on the fatherhood of God is sometimes claimed to be a new teaching. It is, however, foreshadowed in the Old Testament (e.g. v. 5), although the full flowering of this beautiful truth only comes with Jesus, the perfect Son of the Father. The familiar term 'Abba' (Rom. 8:15; Gal. 4:6) is associated in Paul's mind with our position as heirs with Christ. This is also the context here in Deuteronomy where God's disciplining fatherhood (5) leads into the description of Israel's abundant inheritance (7-10).

TO THINK OVER: The dangers of wealth.

Questions for further study and discussion on Deuteronomy 1–8

1. Philippians 4:10-20 is Paul's experience of Deuteronomy 2:7. Discuss in what ways this is or should be true for all Christians.

2. What are the fears which we suffer from today? In what way does Moses' reassurance to Joshua in Deuteronomy 3 also apply to us?

3. For what reasons would the nations envy Israel (Deut. 4:1-8)? What do you find most challenging in this section for your own church in its local community?

4. In what way does 'the Old Testament covenant and law still influence our attitude to God under the new covenant of grace in the blood of Christ' (note on Deut. 5)?

5. 'Teach your children' (6:7) – what does the New Testament say about children of believers? What place should the home have in Christian education?

6. What should be the positive and negative characteristics of a 'people holy to the Lord'?

7. Go through these chapters again and see what they teach about the character of God and his workings.

8. What do these chapters teach about the traditional controversy concerning predestination and human responsibility, election and free will?

9 'Not because of your righteousness'

In the previous chapter Moses affirms that God's blessings to Israel were not due to their greatness or might; now he further declares that they were not the result of their righteousness or uprightness of heart (5). Israel's victories over their neighbours were firstly 'because of the wickedness of these nations' (4) and secondly in fulfilment of the Lord's covenanted promises to their forefathers (5). This chapter underlines the stubbornness, wickedness and sin of God's people (27) and this is illustrated by their rebellious idolatry even at Horeb, where God had manifested himself in fiery glory (7-21), as well as on other occasions (22-24).

God's wrath had been so provoked by Israel's sin that he had been on the point of destroying them (14). Note the implied disowning of Israel by the Lord in the use of 'your' and 'you' in verse 12 – this contrasts with Moses' reminder to God that they were *his* people whom *he* had brought out of Egypt (29). Moses pleaded with God on the basis of his promises to Abraham, Isaac and Jacob (27) and with the supreme motive of the honour of God's name. Moses feared lest the nations should misunderstand God's destruction of Israel (28), causing God's glory to be marred in the sight of the world. Praying and living 'for the Lord's sake' are easier in theory than practice, but the honour of the Lord's name is the supreme motive of the life of the Christian (compare the note on the Ten Commandments).

The threatened destruction of Israel and their replacement by Moses and his family (14) would not have contravened God's covenant with Abraham, for Moses, too, was a descendant of the patriarch.

Twice Moses fasted for forty days and nights in intercession for a rebellious people before mediating the covenant law (18,25). Was this in Jesus' mind as he fasted at the commencement of his teaching and atoning ministry?

Again in this chapter we observe the nature of God as fire (3,15). This fire could illumine and lead Israel by night, but it could also burn with the ferocity of avenging holiness. How right Moses was, therefore, to burn the idolatrous golden calf with fire (21).

FOR MEDITATION: Fire as a symbol of God – what does it say to us about his character and activity?

10 Since, therefore

Von Rad shows the relationship of these chapters to the making of a treaty. In chapter 10 the introduction and historical survey are concluded and this leads into the principal requirements of the treaty outlined in chapter 11. These requirements are given in general (12-21) before their more detailed outworkings (chs. 12-26).

As previously noted, God usually reveals his word through the active participation of men. In the case of the Decalogue, however, he personally wrote on the stone tablets – this is perhaps the origin of the Apocrypha's understanding of heavenly books already in heaven before being revealed to man. This may have influenced Mohammed in his view of the Qur'ān.

The parenthesis beginning in verse 6 should probably close after verse 7 – the use of the third person (6,7) gives way again to the direct second person (9).

Without the other passages concerning the inheritance of the Levites we might conclude from verse 9 that they were left entirely without means. Actually the words 'the Lord is his inheritance' (9) did not exclude the careful provision of cities and pasture lands as well as the system of tithing for their support. Faith in and dependence on the Lord do not necessarily exclude apparently mundane support systems.

On the backdrop of Moses' survey of lessons from history, Israel was faced with God's requirements from her (12-22). The superb summary in verse 12 might stand today as the goal of a Christian's life – reverent fear, loving fellowship with the Lord in obedience and service, total commitment to God. This was followed by the further reminder to keep God's commandments and statutes, for this was 'for your good' (13). Such a righteous walk with the Lord could only stem from a 'circumcised heart' (16, compare Jer. 4:4, Rom. 2:28,29). Such inner transformation was firmly placed in the context of God's loving election (15) and his unique and mighty lordship (17). The primary outworking of a living relationship with such a God was a loving concern for the unfortunate (19) based on the justice of God on behalf of the poor and the defenceless (17,18). Such social concern remained always within the framework of absolute commitment to the Lord alone – you shall fear him, serve him, cleave to him, swear by his name (20), for 'He is your praise; he is your God' (21).

THOUGHT: Faith in and dependence on the Lord do not necessarily exclude apparently mundane support systems.

11 Love and obey

Constant repetition of the warning to obey the Lord in loving submission to his commandments, statutes and ordinances may seem boring and unnecessary to the modern reader. But subsequent history reveals the need for such repeated reminders. Moses knew the weakness of his people and felt deeply the vital importance of following the Lord in total obedience (compare Phil. 3:1).

To reinforce his stern injunctions to the people to keep all the Lord's commandments, Moses cited the stories of God's mighty acts of destruction against the Egyptians and against Dathan and Abiram (3-7). But strict obedience was warmed by the command to 'love the Lord your God' (1).

As Israel prepared for entry into the land of Canaan, Moses not only repeated his words of exhortation, but also gave a permanent visual sign. At the very centre of the new land stood the two mountains of Ebal and Gerizim – Thompson calls them 'the focal point of the promised land'. This was on the way from Shechem to Samaria. It seems that not only were blessing and cursing pronounced from these two mountains, but they represented to the people the reality of God's favour or wrath according to Israel's obedience or idolatry. The sight of these mountains would therefore be a perpetual sermon to the whole people (compare Deut. 27 and Joshua 8:30-35 for further details of the outworking).

The chapter concludes with yet another exhortation to 'do all the statutes and ordinances' (32), for God's blessing was entirely conditional on Israel's obedience (27). Once again we note that the blessing centred particularly on the gift of water and rain (14) while the curse would include the shutting up of the heavens (17). Canaan was a land with abundant water and rainfall as the gift of God ('from heaven', 11); this contrasted with Egypt where Israel had to work hard for the irrigation of the fields (10).

The extent of Israel's inheritance was now measured not only geographically (24b), but also by the promise that 'every place on which the sole of your foot treads shall be yours' (24a) – compare Joshua 1:3; 14:9.

12 A single sanctuary

1. Destruction. The negative preparation for true worship was the total destruction of anything connected with the heathen worship of the Canaanite peoples. Their idols, their holy shrines and their altars were all to be eradicated (2, 3) and Israel was not even to enquire about these practices lest she be ensnared (30). The 'abominable things' were hated by the Lord', for they included such horrifying denials of God's created natural order as child-sacrifice – God had ordained that parents should love and care for their children.

As the name of Yahweh was of central importance, so by contrast the very names of the heathen gods should be wiped out (3) so that their character might not continue to contaminate the land.

The danger for Israel was not only idolatry, but also a syncretistic worship of Yahweh through the use of heathen idolatrous forms – 'you shall not do so to the Lord your God' (4,31). This had been the evil perpetrated by Aaron and the people of Israel when they worshipped Yahweh under the form of the golden calf (compare Deut. 9, Exod. 32) and it continued to plague Israel in the coming years (e.g. Judg. 17).

2. One Sanctuary. The heathen practice of a multitude of shrines was no longer to be allowed in Israel. During the wilderness wanderings there had been no one set place for the worship of the Lord, but in the more settled life in Canaan God would choose one place where all offerings were to be brought. Ordinary animals could be killed and eaten anywhere, but all sacrifices, tithes and offerings should be brought to the place of God's choice. Man would have no part in the selection of the location of God's shrine – God alone would choose.

The worship of God at the central shrine would include the element of joyful fellowship, for eating together formed a vital part of the proceedings (7,18). Israel would rejoice before the Lord in these communal feasts (12,18).

QUESTION: The New Testament church also combined worship with joyful sharing of meals together before the Lord – are we today in danger of losing a biblical pattern in this respect?

13 Enticement to apostasy

Three possible sources of enticement are foreseen in this chapter – the false prophet (1-5), a member of one's own family (6-11) and another city led astray by bad elements in its midst (12-18). In each case the penalty was death (5,9,15,16). Just as the heathen idols and all connected paraphernalia were to be utterly destroyed, so likewise the land and the people of Israel were to be thoroughly purged of any such contaminating influences. Even if the offender were a member of one's immediate family, there was to be no question of pity (8,9). If another city were at fault, it should be entirely destroyed by cleansing and judging fire; no spoil should be kept and the city should never be rebuilt lest its contamination 'cleave to your hand' (17).

False prophets (1-5). Even if the prophet had given evidence of spiritual power through the use of a sign or miracle which came to pass, still his words and visions were to be judged by the higher standard of God's word and commandments. Dreams, visions and miracles are not necessarily signs of truth.

Family enticement (6-11). The agony of choice between family love and obedience to the Lord is foreseen, but personal sentiment and home ties must not be placed above our loyalty to God. Where necessary we must forsake even our closest and most loved family, for the Lord and his commandments are supreme.

In discussing the case of the false prophet Moses did not specify what forms of idolatry were in question. But here he widened the horizons of false religion to include even the philosophies and religions which came from far-off lands. In today's world many are enticed by the romanticism and mystique of oriental faiths, but the man of God is against both local idolatries and also those from afar (7).

The purpose behind the destruction of those guilty of leading Israel astray was twofold. Firstly it was to 'purge the evil from the midst of you' (5) in order that the land and society might not be contaminated by the corrupting evil. Secondly it acted as a deterrent, that 'all Israel shall hear, and fear, and never again do any such wickedness' (11). In a righteous criminal code how should the reform of the criminal relate to these two principles?

14 Laws on mourning, eating and tithing

In the Hebrew the expressions 'sons' and 'holy people' (1,2) are placed in the emphatic first position in their respective sentences. These two aspects of Israel's relationship with Yahweh form the basis of the ensuing commandments. The intimacy of sonship and the sanctity of being God's unique people precluded any defiling activity. Mutilation of the body in mourning (1,2) not only had pagan significance but also demonstrated a lack of true respect for the body as God's creation and possession (compare 2 Cor. 6:16; 7:1).

Israel's calling to be God's holy people was further exemplified by the food laws (3-21). Whereas the sabbath laws were for the sake of the Gentiles in Israel's midst and therefore applied also to the Gentiles, the food laws demonstrated Israel's unique position as God's chosen people and therefore did not apply to foreigners (21). The forbidden mourning customs and the food laws are almost exact repetitions of Leviticus 19:28 and Leviticus 11 respectively.

The prohibitions against boiling a kid in its mother's milk (21) may possibly have been in opposition to a fertility rite described in the Ugaritic texts, although the Ugaritic poem does not specify the *mother's* milk. The Mishnah expounds this verse as requiring separation of meat and milk foods (Hullin 8.4).

Harvest festivities could easily turn into Canaanite fertility rites, so careful instructions were given that all tithes and first fruits (there is some discussion about whether these are the same or different offerings) should be brought to the central shrine of Yahweh's choice. The celebration feast was not to be eaten elsewhere but must be celebrated 'before the Lord your God' (26). If it was too far to bring the offerings in kind, then they could be exchanged for money and then food and drink bought in Jerusalem (24-26). Every three years the tithe was to be kept in each home town and used for the maintenance of the Levites, the poor and the needy. For the relationship of these ordinances with the tithe laws in Numbers 18, see Thompson in *Deuteronomy* (Tyndale Commentary). In practice, the tithe seems to have been used largely for the maintenance of the Temple and its priestly servants and for the support of the needy, with only a small part going to the communal feast. We note again that piety did not necessarily include teetotalism (26).

FOR MEDITATION: Our calling as 'sons' and 'holy people'.

15 The year of release

The previous chapter ends with the commandment to generosity in obedience to the Lord's commandments; if Israel followed the Lord's statutes, God would bless them (14:28-29). Now this chapter continues the same theme. Prosperity was promised to Israel (4,6) if they followed God's commandments for the year of release. Liberality of spirit should not allow a failure to provide for the needs of a poor Israelite (7-11). The Hebrew slave should not only be released at the seventh year, but should also be sent away with a generous gift of cattle and food (12-18). Such generosity would result in the Lord's blessing (18).

This principle that God rewards with material blessing the generosity of his children is also found in the New Testament (2 Cor. 9:6,11; Phil. 4:17,19). God never leaves himself debtor to his children, but always gives to us more than we give to others – it should however be said that sometimes his rewards are spiritual rather than material.

Moses foresaw the ideal society which God desired for his people. One aspect of the repeated 'the Lord will bless you' is that 'there will be no poor among you' (4) – what a contrast with the actual outworking in historical fact (Matt. 26:11). The existence of poverty is an offence against God's perfect will for society. Debt to Gentiles was forbidden to Israel, although she might lend to them. Usury among Jews was not allowed (23:19), but with Gentiles it was permitted. Debt always involves economic power and the possibility of manipulation of the debtor, so it is here linked with God's desire that Israel should never be ruled over by Gentiles (6). Again, the consequences of Israel's sin were to make reality a far cry from God's ideal.

At the year of release there might be some slaves who refused the offer of freedom. They could then be marked with a hole in the ear and become perpetual slaves – the term 'bondman for ever' (17) is also found in Ugaritic literature where it seems to imply a person of some significance and is by no means a derogatory term. Preachers have frequently used these verses to demonstrate the Christian's voluntary and eternal submission to the Lord he loves.

CHALLENGE: The existence of poverty is an offence against God's perfect will for society.

16:1-17 The three great feasts

1. Passover (1-8). Again the emphasis here is that each of the feasts was to be celebrated 'at the place which the Lord will choose'. Three times a year the whole people of Israel were to congregate at the Lord's chosen place to worship and celebrate in unity together. Such focal points in the nation's life of worship cemented their oneness as a people in communion with their God.

A key symbolic feature of the Passover feast was the removal of all leaven. Unleavened bread became the basic food (3) and no leaven was to be found in all their territory (4) – today's Jews search and sweep their houses to ensure that no leaven remains. The lack of leaven symbolised the haste of their last meal before the flight from Egypt; leaven later became a picture of sin. Whether the Last Supper was a Passover celebration or just a Sabbath preparation meal is not certain, but it is sure that in either case no leaven will have been used in that evening meal. It is strange that the Christian church has made the external details of the Sacrament of Baptism a matter of bitter controversy, while flagrantly ignoring biblical practice by the use of leavened bread and the celebration of the Sacrament of the Lord's Supper in the morning – let alone the failure to recline in the manner evidently practised in the New Testament. It is, however, the spiritual significance of the Passover which is highlighted in this chapter.

2. The Feast of Weeks/Pentecost (9-12). The Feast of Weeks celebrated the gathering of the harvest and took place fifty days (hence 'Pentecost') from the Sabbath beginning the Passover. Here it is counted as seven weeks from the commencement of harvesting the grain (9). Its hallmark was the gift of a freewill offering to the Lord and a joyful feast together. This celebration in remembrance of Israel's own former servitude in Egypt was shared with the servants, religious workers and defenceless members of society (11,14).

3. Booths (13-15). This great feast was also associated with the gathering in of the harvest. Thompson suggests that it particularly celebrated the fruit harvest, although the 'threshing floor' is also mentioned. We notice God's purpose for his people that they 'will be altogether joyful' (15), compare John 15:11, 1 John 1:4.

QUESTION: What focal points in the lives of our churches cement our oneness as a people in communion with our God?

16:18-17:20 Justice under God

In the early days Moses had administered justice alone, but here in preparation for life in Canaan he reminded Israel to appoint judges and leaders for each town (16:18). He was concerned that Israel's national life should be based on justice through an incorrupt judiciary. Righteous justice must not be perverted by partiality or bribery. Many countries today know the consequences of corrupt judges or a judiciary under the sway of governments or other power groups. The welfare of a nation depends very much on a just legal system.

Justice in a theocracy relates also to the great sin of idolatry (17:2-7) and therefore Moses gave yet another warning to worship the Lord alone (16:21,22) and to do so with right sacrifices (17:1). No idolatry or nature worship was to be countenanced in Israel (3). As the avenger of blood was the first to execute justice on the murderer (Num. 35:19), so here the witnesses led the execution of the idolater (7) – this provision further discouraged false witnesses. Evidence must be supported by more than one witness.

Provision was made for difficult cases with which local judges might not feel adequate to deal (8-13). If appeal was made to higher authorities, their decision should be binding (10-13) for it came from 'before the Lord your God' (12).

God himself was King over Israel in the theocracy, but Moses foresaw Israel's demand for a human king like the surrounding nations (14). Whereas 1 Samuel 8 shows the evil results of such a denial of the divine kingship, this chapter allows Israel to proceed with the choice of a king and advises what sort of man they should select. He was to be the man of God's choice (15) and not a foreigner. These two conditions fitted the role of Israel as God's holy people. Despotic power was prohibited in Israel. Even the king was to be subject to the greater authority of God's law, so that he might learn to 'fear the Lord his God' and be obedient to his word. Humility should mark the king's character as 'one from among your brethren' whose 'heart may not be lifted up above his brethren'. The dangers of pride were paralleled by the snare of greed. The king was not to 'multiply horses' for himself (16), nor was he to compromise God's will for Israel for the sake of national wealth. The multiplication of wives was closely related to the multiplication of silver and gold (17). The enticements of women, as Solomon discovered, could easily introduce an idolatrous decline.

Questions for further study and discussion on Deuteronomy 9–17

1. On what occasions did Moses and Jesus fast (see note on Deut. 9)? Discuss the place of fasting for the Christian today.

2. Deuteronomy 12:2,3 commands complete destruction of evil religious beliefs from the land and from the mind (compare Phil. 4:8). How do we decide when to study other beliefs and sects, and when to leave them completely alone? What is the apostolic attitude to other religions?

3. The Israelite religion was characterised by celebrations and 'joyful feasts' (see note on Deut. 16). How does the church express its joy before the Lord?

4. When members of the church today prophesy or give a message from God, how do we decide its validity? (See Deut. 13, also 1 John 4:1-3.)

5. 'Strict justice must be your ideal' (16:18). Go through these chapters again to see God's concern for justice. How should this apply to our society?

6. In what ways are we often unjust in our individual lives?

7. Moses used past history to instruct Israel for the present and future. See how the New Testament does the same (e.g. Acts 7; Heb. 11). What use should we make of history?

8. Note again the required characteristics for Israel's king (17:14-20). Apply these standards to today's leaders in church and society (including ourselves in whatever sphere of leadership we may be called to).

18 Priests, Levites, magicians and prophets

The support of priests and Levites (1-8). The RSV by its unwarranted insertion of 'that is' (1) wrongly equates the priests with 'all the tribe of Levi', whereas it seems that only a part of the tribe served as priests. However, there was to be no differentiation between the priests and the Levites: to ensure this, any Levite could leave his provincial ministry at any time to share in the life and work of the priests in 'the place which the Lord will choose' (6). Here he would share equal provision with his fellow Levites. As in previous chapters, it is made clear again here that the Levites should not have a full inheritance like other tribes, but should live from the offerings and tithes of the people. The labourer is worthy of his hire (Luke 10:7).

Magic and the occult (9-14). All forms of occult practice are condemned here in the strongest possible terms. Israel was not to take over from the surrounding nations their heathen attempts to manipulate the spirits, contact the dead or determine the future. The exhaustive list of forbidden arts expressly excludes every occult activity, whether it comes into the category of magic or into the realm of contact with the spirits. Soothsayers and fortune-tellers are included as 'abominations'. Israel (14) was to be utterly different from the surrounding nations, for she was called to be 'blameless before the Lord your God'. It was because of such evil practices that God was driving the nations out of Canaan and allowing Israel to replace them; if Israel followed their example she would suffer the same penalty.

A Prophet to come (15-22). At Horeb Israel had rightly demanded a man to mediate God's words to them. Moses was God's answer and now his successor would likewise act as God's prophet to Israel. But this section looks beyond the immediate and partial fulfilment to the coming messianic prophet who would perfectly speak God's words and 'all that I command him' (18).

Verse 21 is a most apposite question for all ages – how can we know when a prophetic word is from God? The answer here is simple – wait and see whether it comes true (22).

TO THINK OVER: What is the special relevance of verses 9-14 in our society?

Cities of Refuge

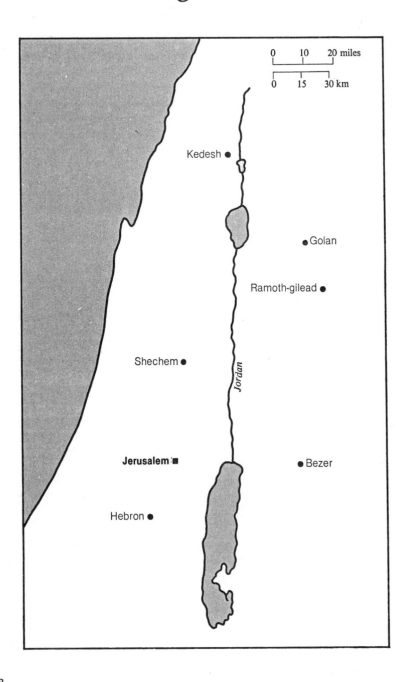

19 Protection for the vulnerable

Cities of Refuge (1-13). Numbers 35 has already dealt in some detail with the question of the cities of refuge. Moses here adds the administrative provision of roads (3) and gives a graphic illustration of manslaughter (5). The selection of the three cities east of Jordan was, as far as we know, never completed by the appointment of the other three cities in Canaan itself. This was perhaps due to the failure of Israel to fulfil her side of the covenant with the result that God never gave the totality of the promised land. The 'if' of verse 8 looms large because of Israel's sin (9).

The big addition to the provisions of Numbers 35 is the word 'innocent' (10,13). It was the shedding of *innocent* blood which defiled the land. Therefore the murder of a man who accidentally committed manslaughter or the failure to 'purge the guilt of innocent blood' through the just execution of a murderer was an offence against the Lord. Is this principle still valid for today's debate on capital punishment?

The landmark (14). This follows immediately after the question of murder, for there is a close connection between a man's land as his means of support and the actual life of that man. To defraud him through the removal of a landmark did him grievous harm. A man's inheritance was sacrosanct, for it was 'the land that the Lord your God gives you to possess'.

Laws of evidence (15-21). Once again Moses repeats his requirement that no charge should be upheld on the evidence of one person only. Here he adds a further word on dealing with a false witness. Such a serious crime was to be tested before the Lord and the highest authorities in the land (17). After diligent enquiry, if the witness was indeed found to be false, then verse 19 came into effect. The so-called 'Lex Talionis' was applied in Exodus and Leviticus for the repayment of damage done to another in a quarrel (Exod. 21:23-25; Lev. 24:20), but here it is applied according to the hurtful intentions of the false witness. Jesus widens the application of the principle (Matt. 5:38-42) and adds his own 'but I say unto you'. Again the purpose of these regulations was that they should be deterrents so that false witness might not become a national habit.

20 Fear not!

'**The Lord your God is with you**' (1-9). Despite the daunting sight of the enemy's more powerful forces (1) Israel was not to fear. Note the number of different words used in this passage to describe fear – Israel knew the paralysing reality of this temptation. The antidote was twofold. Firstly, the people were to realise the reality of God's mighty presence with them; he went with them, fought for them and gave them the victory. The battle was therefore not between Israel and her enemies – it was between God and the armies of the heathen. Secondly, Israel was not to take into battle men whose hearts might not be prepared for courageous self-sacrifice in battle, lest their faintheartedness be infectious (8). The man with a new house, vineyard or wife should not go into battle until he had had time to enjoy them. God understands the natural desires of the human heart and makes due allowance. The principles of verses 5-7 apply to active Christian service today.

While the general principle of fearless trust in the Lord was stated by the priest (2), the more specific outworkings (5-8) were enunciated by the more local 'officers' (5). Only then were the more senior 'commanders' appointed (9).

Waging war (10-20). The cruelties of genocidal annihilation were to be avoided if possible when dealing with those cities which were 'very far from you'. Peace (10) was preferable to war. But if they insisted on war, then victory was assured (13). All men were to be killed, but women and children, cattle and booty might be taken as spoil. The situation was totally different with the Canaanite nations (16-18). They were ripe for judgement and their continued existence would endanger the moral and spiritual life of Israel (18). Peace terms were not to be offered, for 'utterly destroy' was God's commandment to Israel.

Even an extended siege did not make total warfare allowable (19,20). Some trees might be used for war purposes, but the land was not to be stripped of the fruit-bearing trees. The natural environment may not be sacrificed for military purposes – trees are not men to be besieged (19)!

QUESTION: What should we think of modern methods of warfare in the light of these verses?

21 Keep the land holy!

Innocent blood (1-9, 22,23). Further commandments are here given on how to prevent the contamination of the land through the shedding of innocent blood. If it could not be atoned for through the judgement of the murderer, then the nearest city was responsible for asserting its innocence (7) and had prayerfully to sacrifice a heifer to win forgiveness for the people of Israel and to purge the land of guilt. This was to be done through the mediation of the priests, the sons of Levi, for they had the divine commission to minister, to bless and to settle disputes (5).

If, however, the man guilty of a capital crime was known and duly executed, the land was not to be defiled through the dead body left hanging from the tree (22,23). God's curse rested on the man who was hung in this way. Note Paul's use of this truth in his explanation of the work of Jesus Christ on the cross (Gal. 3:13). He became accursed of God for our sake, although he was not guilty of any death-deserving sin. The Jews were careful not to contaminate the land by allowing the crucified bodies to remain hanging, but they had no hesitation in killing the sinless Jesus and thus shedding innocent blood. But how wonderful for us that the curse of our sin has been paid by Jesus!

Family holiness (10-21). Although the Israelite was allowed to take a captive Gentile woman to be his wife, he was not permitted to treat her shamefully (10-14). She could not be kept as a mere concubine with no rights, but became a wife with the same rights as her Jewish equivalent (24:1-4). The man had the right to divorce his wife, but she could not be sold back into slavery.

Polygamy, with its usual complications, was evidently not unusual (15). Favouritism spoiled the lives of the patriarchs and Moses here legislated for righteous treatment of the child of the unloved wife (15-17). Unrighteousness in the home offends a holy God. A consistently rebellious and disobedient son who rejects parental discipline is a threat to an ordered society. His parents were to bring such to the elders at the city gate, the place of judgement. Death through stoning would purge the land of this corrupting evil. We today are in danger of losing an appreciation of the depth of sin involved in disobedience to parents.

22 Miscellaneous social and sexual laws

Social (1-4, 6-12). These next four chapters contain a number of laws in no particular order, although sometimes related ordinances are grouped together (e.g. 13-30). God's law reaches into every aspect of life and affects all relationships with man (e.g. 1-4,8) and with our natural environment (e.g. 9,10).

Assisting one's neighbour in time of need is no optional act of charity, but a requirement of the Law – 'you may not withhold your help' (3). Even if such help involved the cost of feeding and caring for the lost beast (1,2), obligation to help is laid upon us. Passive inaction is sin. Precautionary measures for the safety of others are also required (8).

Purity and unsullied holiness are basic principles underlying all the law. This not only involved prohibitions against intermarriage with heathen men and syncretistic worship of Canaanite deities, but the principle of purity carried over into agricultural pursuits (9,10) and clothing (11). It seems that the picture of a mixed plough team lay before Paul's eyes in 2 Corinthians 6:14. These verses of detailed application of the basic principle of holiness led naturally to the requirement that a reminder of God's law be visibly worn to ensure that Israel 'remember and do all my commandments and be holy to your God' (Num. 15:37-41).

Sexual (5,13-30). Verse 5 condemns transvestite perversion, but does not specify what forms of clothing pertain to each sex; that is a cultural detail which varies from nation to nation and generation to generation.

Social stability and morality depend on the basic family unit. Marital and sexual disorder can pervade and wreck a nation like a cancer, so God decreed death to be the penalty for pre-marital sex (20,21), adultery (22), voluntary intercourse with another man by a betrothed virgin (23,24) and rape (25-27). Marriage could expurgate the sin of extra-marital sex where neither party was engaged or married (28,29). Divorce was then not permitted as an escape (19,29).

We note that betrothal was considered tantamount to marriage (23,24 compare Matt. 1:19). In Jewish culture engagement was not lightly entered into and required an official act of divorce to break it.

THOUGHT: Assisting one's neighbour in time of need is no optional act of charity, but a requirement of the law.

23 'Keep yourself from every evil thing'

A holy assembly (1-8) The assembly (*Qahal*) signified the covenant people of God with particular reference to them as a worshipping community. Entry into the assembly therefore implied full acceptance with religious as well as social privileges and responsibilities. The community included aliens, but they were not part of the *Qahal*. The castration referred to here (1) probably does not refer to accident or illness, but to purposeful mutilation connected with heathen rites (see also 17,18). The rare word for 'bastard' (*mamzer*) may well refer to children of incestuous marriages – note that 22:29 would restrict the number of other illegitimate children.

The prohibition 'to the tenth generation' against the Ammonites and Moabites did not extend to the more closely related Edomites and Egyptians, for whom it was only until the third generation (8). In the light of more recent history it is interesting that Israel was not to 'abhor' an Egyptian (7) – the word 'abhor' has the same root as the noun 'abomination', implying God's just loathing of the corrupt; it is the direct opposite of that loving kindness (Heb. *chesed*) which characterises the covenant relationship.

The law against the Moabites (3) evidently still allowed for and spotlighted the exercise of grace (compare the case of Ruth).

Camp purity (9-14). Hygiene and holiness interlock in these very practical ordinances, but the overriding principle is found in verse 14. What a text for the life of God's people today also!

A medley of commandments (15-25). Generous kindliness in brotherly and neighbourly relations underlay the treatment of the runaway slave (15,16), the lending of money (19,20) and the permission to eat freely when walking in a neighbour's vineyard or grain field (24,25). This contrasts vividly with the Hammurabi Code which made death the penalty for harbouring a runaway slave.

God's word in the Old Testament is powerful and produces results. So also man's word should be taken seriously. A promise or vow must be turned into action. The utterance of a promise was considered to be a vow to the Lord (23) – compare Acts 5:1-11.

24 Justice and kindness

The RSV corrects the AV of verse 1 in discouraging divorce by making remarriage of one's formerly divorced wife illegal. This was aimed against both hasty divorce and any possibility of lending a wife temporarily to another man. Divorce is here a possibility if the wife lost favour with her husband 'because he has found some indecency in her' (1). What this 'indecency' may have been is unclear (compare 23:14). Matthew 19:9 seems to assume that it refers to 'unchastity', but the emphasis of Jesus' words is on the fact that remarriage is tantamount to committing adultery or to making the divorced wife commit adultery by remarriage (compare Mark 10:11,12). It is clear from Christ's teaching that divorce is only permitted in the Mosaic Law 'because of the hardness of your hearts' and is highly undesirable in the congregation of God's people.

Generous attitudes to the newly married (5, compare 20:7) and to the defenceless poor (6,7,10-22) are fundamental to godly living. The basic means of living might not be taken from the poor in payment of debt, for this was like 'taking a life' (6) and it might lead to the poor crying to the Lord against the creditor (15). Oppressive adherence to strict legality was forbidden, for mercy with justice and kindness were more important than a man's financial rights. Thus it was true that a man's crop belonged totally to him, but in mercy he had to leave the gleanings for 'the sojourner, the fatherless, and the widow' (19-21). Likewise a debt should legally be paid, but not if this involved undue suffering for the poor (6,10-13).

The weak in society were in no way to be mistreated. The poor hired worker should be given his wage on time, for he depended upon it (14,15). Justice should not be perverted against the poor and powerless (17,18), for the Israelites were never to forget their former position as slaves in Egypt.

The doctrine of personal responsibility was further developed by Ezekiel (16, compare Ezek. 18) and then became a basic tenet of the Pharisees and of the Christian church. The Bible does teach a corporate responsibility; and judgement or blessing does descend from one generation to another, but still each individual remains personally accountable for his actions.

25 Miscellaneous laws

Forty stripes (1-3). The aim of this regulation was the prevention of unduly severe beatings which might degrade – Israel was never to forget that the criminal was still her 'brother'. Punishment was graded to fit the crime (compare Luke 12:47,48). Tradition reduced the maximum penalty to thirty-nine to safeguard those who administered the beating, lest they miscount (compare 2 Cor. 11:24).

The muzzled ox (4). This verse stands alone without parallel in the Mosaic Law, but care for the servant and the powerless has the same underlying principle. The one who works to produce food deserves a share of the harvest. Paul develops this law to prove the right of Christian workers to live from the fruit of their labours. The church is responsible for the payment of its workers and for giving them the honour due to them (1 Cor. 9:9; 1 Tim. 5:18).

Levirate marriage (5-10). This custom was not exclusive to Israel, for it was practised also by the Assyrians and Hittites. The fear of dying without the possibility of one's name living on through one's sons still remains an anxiety in many cultures today. The Bible refers several times to this practice (Gen. 38:8; Mark 12:18-27 and the story of Ruth). Jesus' ancestry therefore twice includes a background of levirate marriage: through Er (Gen. 38; Luke 3:28) and Ruth.

Indecency (11,12). This is the only Old Testament example of mutilation being prescribed, whereas in the Hammurabi and Assyrian Codes it was quite normal. Through this severe penalty the sacrosanct privacy of their reproductive organs was maintained even in a fight where the woman was attempting to rescue her husband.

Honesty (13-16). If Israel wished to remain in her God-given land, she had to deal honestly in business affairs. Double-dealing and shady commercial practice 'are an abomination to the Lord' and would result in Israel's expulsion from her inheritance. As with so many of God's commandments, Israel in fact flouted this law (Amos 8:5). In these days of business corruption the principle of a 'full and just measure' may be widely and pertinently applied.

Amalek (17-19). In the Old Testament nations are normally condemned for their mistreatment of Israel, their corrupt religious practices and their immoral conduct. It is rare, however, that a nation is condemned not only for these evils, but also because they 'did not fear God' (18).

26 Offering the first fruits

On taking possession of the promised land Israel was to engage in a solemn act of thanksgiving and dedication. This centred in the offering of the first fruits to the Lord, declarations of what God had done for them and the continuing relationship between Israel and Yahweh. The offering of the first fruits (compare Lev. 23:9-14) reminded Israel that the land and its harvests came from the bountiful hand of God. His grace supplied every good gift; all belonged to him; all was to be enjoyed in obedient subservience to him.

Entry into the promised land formed a watershed in the experience of the people. Reflection on the past introduced a forward-looking determination to continue in obedience to God's commandments. Israel looked back to their ancestor Jacob, the 'wandering Aramean' (5), and his descent into Egypt with all its consequences of affliction and slavery. But Egypt was also the place where God made Israel into a nation (5) and where Israel saw the Lord answering their cries of despair. Suffering – agonised prayer – signs and wonders (8) – a land flowing with milk and honey (9) – bringing the first of the fruit (10) – worship (10). What a significant succession of events!

But worship was not the end of the chain of events. It led directly to a renewal of the covenant relationship with the Lord (16-19). Note the repeated 'this day' (3,16-19) which underlines the progression from the thankful offering of the first fruits to the solemn declarations by Israel (17) and by Yahweh (18,19). Both declarations renewed the relationship of Israel as God's people and possession; both asserted Israel's role in keeping all God's commandments and so walking in his ways. In addition the Lord promised to set Israel 'high above all nations' to be praised and honoured by all around them. Israel should be a 'people holy to the Lord' – this was the climax of the covenant, for it implied not only that Yahweh alone would be Israel's God but also that God would bless Israel above all others.

THOUGHT: The tithe was given partly to the Levites and partly to the needy (12). Christian giving today should support the poor as well as Christian work and workers.

Questions for further study and discussion on Deuteronomy 18–26

1. What would you say to someone who says, 'I see no harm in reading the stars' (Deut. 18:9-14)?

2. God made sure that the priests and Levites had provision for all their needs (Deut. 18:1-8). Our pastors and clergy have particular emotional and spiritual needs as well as material needs. To what extent do we care for their needs? Is there anything further we could do?

3. How may we today discern the voice of the Lord (see 18:21,22)?

4. One of the hardest of all commands is the command to love those who are mean, unfair and disagreeable to us (Matt. 5:38-42; note on Deut. 19). Discuss how this can be achieved.

5. Chapter 20 talked much of fear; look up this word in a concordance to see what the New Testament says about it. What things are we afraid of? Why?

6. How do we decide how to allocate the money we set aside for God's work (Deut. 26)?

7. We are obliged to help those in need. 'Passive inaction is sin' (compare Matt. 25:31-46). We are surrounded by so many needs – how can we decide what to do?

8. Do a careful study of the relevant passages on divorce (see note on Deut. 24).

9. Work through these chapters again and observe their relevance for living in society today.

27 Mount Ebal and the recitation of curses

Editorial arrangement of the words of Moses is evidenced here by the reference to Moses in the third person (1,9,11, compare 5:1). This continues through the following chapters (e.g. 29:1; 31:1,30; 32:44, etc.), up to the climactic final chapter where the story of Moses' death is obviously not written by himself.

Deuteronomy generally stresses God's choice of one central place for worship and sacrifice in opposition to multitudinous local shrines where worship could so easily degenerate into Canaanite fertility rites. In this chapter, however, Israel is commanded to build an altar and offer sacrifices at Mount Ebal on the west bank of the Jordan. It may be that this was merely for the renewal of the Sinai covenant on entry into Canaan (note the parallel between vs. 5,6 and Exod. 20:25) and would cease to serve as an altar of sacrifice after the central shrine had been chosen. We note that Mount Ebal was close to Shechem, the location of the central sanctuary in early Israel (Josh. 24:1).

We observe again the importance God gives to outward and visible reminders of his gracious promises and of 'the words of this law' (2-4). As so often in Deuteronomy the offering of sacrifice was inseparably linked to ceremonial eating together and rejoicing before the Lord (7).

The future orientation of this chapter (2-8, 12-26) remains firmly anchored to Israel's present obligations – note the repeated 'this day' (1,9,10) as in chapter 26 and 28:1. True religion remembers the past and hopes for the future, but all must be of relevance to the present.

For the cursing and blessing of Mounts Gerizim and Ebal, see 11:26-32. The curses follow a logical order, beginning with the supreme sin of idolatry (15), followed naturally by disobedience to parents (16), social injustice and unrighteousness (17-19), sexual perversion (20-23) and finally secret or underhand methods of 'slaying his neighbour' (24,25). These are finally summarised by the general curse of verse 26. To each curse all the people responded with a solemn Amen. The repetition of 'all' underlined the responsibility of every member of the people of God – and the repeated 'Amen' must have made a vivid impression upon them all.

THOUGHT: True religion remembers the past and hopes for the future, but all must be of relevance to the present.

28 'If you obey . . . will not obey'

Moses spelt out the blessings attached to careful obedience to God's commandments (1-14) and the fearful consequences of disobedience (15-68). The ideal picture of God's saving word for Israel was always the impressive sequence of mighty works associated with the Exodus from Egypt, so here the climax of God's curse and judgement on Israel was a return to Egypt for further slavery – but with the greater shame that no one would want such degraded people as slaves (68).

Israel was tempted to follow the fertility rites of the heathen nations in order to gain fruitfulness of body, cattle and land. God forestalled this by promising precisely these blessings if Israel would be obedient (4,5,11), whereas his curse would rob them of such fruitfulness (18).

Moses recognised the distinction between life in the city and in the country (3,16). On entry into the promised land Israel would begin to face the situations involved in urban life. God's promises and curses applied to both, for he is not merely an agricultural fertility god.

The purpose and high point of God's blessing on Israel was that the surrounding nations should see that the Lord was with them and should therefore come to fear the power of the Lord in them (10). Likewise God's curse would result in Israel becoming a 'horror, a proverb, and a byword among all the peoples' (37) and in Israel serving her enemies (48) instead of the nations serving God's people. The picture of prosperity and peaceful settled life in fertile Canaan would be replaced by the curse of exile. Israel would be led away by a nation 'from afar' (49) which spoke a 'language you do not understand'. The fearful horrors of famine in a besieged city were guaranteed to shock (53-57) – but even more distressing was the fact that God actually delighted in bringing the ruin of judgement upon his people (63) because they trusted in their own strength (52) and did not 'serve the Lord your God with joyfulness' (47) and therefore they would serve their enemies (48) and would be scattered among all peoples (64).

TO THINK OVER: How do our individual lives and church lives reflect the power and glory of our God?

29 Covenant renewal

This chapter sees the start of Moses' third address (compare 1:1; 4:44). How it fits into the overall structure of the book of Deuteronomy remains a matter for debate, but clearly the outline is patterned on the political treaties of the ancient Near East. A historical prologue (1:6–3:29) is followed by a summary of basic commandments (4:1-40; 5:1–11:32) which are then made specific (12:1–26:19). Then comes the statement of blessings and curses in general (27:1-26) and in greater detail (28:1-68). Finally the whole is summarised and restated (29:1–30:20).

A restatement of the covenant and its consequences was necessitated by the obdurate blindness of Israel (4) which continued to characterise the later history of Israel (Isa. 6:9-13; Matt. 13:14,15; Acts 28:26-28). Israel had no excuse for not knowing that Yahweh was truly 'the Lord your God' (6), for she had witnessed an amazing catalogue of miracles at the Exodus and in the years of wandering in the wilderness. Experience of God's wonderful working brings with it responsibility to follow him obediently (9).

Neglect of the Lord and his commandments produced complacent self-assurance which smiled at God's threats of judgement (19). Irreligion and idolatry contaminate like a cancerous root which produces a harvest of poison and bitterness (18; Acts 8:23; Heb. 12:15). God could not ignore such sin. His judgement would strike 'moist and dry alike' – the sinners and their innocent compatriots would suffer as one people together.

Israel's obedience and consequent blessing should have demonstrated God's glory before the eyes of the surrounding nations. Whatever Israel's behaviour, God remained determined that these nations should take note of the power and righteousness of Yahweh. 'Therefore' (27) God's anger would be kindled and he would devastate the land (23).

Some aspects of God's character and working remain a mystery to mortal men, but sufficient is revealed to lay upon us and our children the responsibility to 'do all the words of this law' (29). It is healthy for us all to remember that we only know a small portion of the deep riches of God. It is also helpful to be reminded that God's revelation must result in obedient action. And what God has revealed shall be passed on to our children from one generation to another for ever.

30 'With all your heart'

The law is given to man as a means of life. Total obedience to God's commandments merits life and blessing (16; 5:33). Sadly, however, the corruption of the human heart makes this route to salvation a dead end. Therefore the previous chapter majored on the consequences of disobedience, rather than expanding on the glories of blessing. The banishment threatened in those verses leads on in this chapter to repentance and a return to the Lord (1,2). God will then restore Israel to her own land and will shower his blessings on the people (3-5).

Repentance and the Lord's restoration of Israel to the promised land could only lead to further sin against God's law unless God radically changed the basic nature of the people. Experiencing the tragic realities of Israel's captivity, Jeremiah and Ezekiel knew the necessity of a new heart (Jer. 31:33; Ezek. 36:26). Therefore God promised that he 'will circumcise your heart' to the end that Israel may be able to 'love the Lord your God' and so live (6). Fulfilment of the Law is found in this fundamental command to love the Lord. This introduces a new sequence of God's actions in and for Israel: circumcision of the heart – love of the Lord – defeat of Israel's enemies (7) – obedience (8) – God's delight in prospering his people (9). Obedience to God's commandments remains central to the life of God's people, but now it results from God's work in changing the human heart and it ceases to be the condition for life. Jesus, too, sees obedience as the necessary consequence of love (John 14:15) while John shows it to be a hallmark of the Christian life which therefore gives assurance that we know the Lord (1 John 2:3).

Due to the gracious working of God in the heart (6), the words of God are 'not too hard' (11) for they are even 'in your heart'. It was on this basis that Moses made his moving appeal to choose between life and death (15-20). Paul develops this thought of the life-giving word of righteousness through faith; it is offered as the way to salvation for all who will call upon the name of the Lord (Rom. 10:5-12). Faith and salvation can only come through hearing the word of life, so Paul urges the necessity of Christians being sent to preach to 'Jew and Greek', to all peoples.

31 'Be strong . . . I will be with you'

The end approaches for Moses. After this chapter it only remained for him to recite his final song (ch. 32), declare his blessings upon the children of Israel (ch. 33) and ascend the mountain of his death (ch. 34). A new era under the leadership of Joshua was beginning; Canaan lay before the people with all its rich blessings, its battles and its pagan temptations. A new stage in the life of a Christian or of a church always contains blessings, battles and temptations.

Moses' confidence in leadership rested on the knowledge that God himself was with him as the absolute King and Leader of the people. Joshua now and all Israel with him could enjoy the same assurance. Moses addressed the same words to Joshua and to all Israel (6-8). Courage and strength issued from the knowledge that the Lord went with them and before them. God would never fail nor forsake his people. Joshua and his people could therefore face the battles and temptations without fear. God reminded Joshua of Moses' words when commissioning him to lead the people across Jordan (Josh. 1:5-9).

Moses left behind him two witnesses to remind Israel of God's commandments and the consequent blessings or curses. Firstly, he taught them a song (19-22) – meaningful hymns and choruses have always been significant witnesses to God's people. Secondly, Moses made sure that the 'book of the law' should be kept before the people in the ark of the covenant (24-26) and should be read to all the people in solemn assembly during the year of release (9-13). The centrality of the written word of God is vital for the spiritual health of God's people.

We notice a striking similarity between the commissioning of Joshua and Jesus' great commission to his disciples (Matt. 28:16-20). The fact that some of the disciples doubted, parallels Joshua's evident temptation to fear. The remedy of 'all authority in heaven and on earth' is reminiscent of the Lord who 'will go over before you; he will destroy these nations' (3): to Joshua and the disciples the Lord promises 'I will be with you' (23). As Joshua brought Israel into the promised land, so Jesus' followers 'go and make disciples of all nations', bringing them into the promises of God.

32 The song of Moses

Heaven and earth were called to bear witness to the solemnity of this song (31:28; 32:1) and its testimony to the people of Israel. Its purpose is stated to be the ascription of praise to the name of Yahweh (3). This great aim is fulfilled in the following verses with their declaration of God's ways as perfect, just, faithful and without iniquity (4) in stark contrast to Israel's dealings which were corrupt, blemished, perverse and crooked (5). The 'foolish and senseless' people of Israel are contrasted with the Lord whose fatherly care lavished love, protection, gentle guidance and munificent provision on Israel (6-14).

The riches of God's blessings made Israel 'fat' and 'sleek' (15; 31:20) with the sad result that Israel forsook, provoked and scoffed at their Creator who is the 'Rock of their salvation' (15,16). The pathos of Israel turning from the source of all their blessings is underlined by the repeated affirmation of God's uniqueness. 'There is no god beside me' (39). He alone can kill or make alive, wound or heal. Israel thought religion was an optional extra, but Moses stated categorically that 'it is no trifle for you, but it is your life' (47). The restrained but wrathful justice of verse 21 should have warned Israel of the fearful folly of turning from the Lord to demons (17), idols (21) and gods which were foreign to Israel (16,17) and totally inferior to Yahweh (37-42). The fact that Yahweh is unique and incomparable relates closely to our modern questions about the relationship of the Christian faith to other religions. Moses would have objected strongly to the idea that all roads lead to Rome or to Mt. Fuji (for further study of this subject, see the author's *Don't Just Stand There*, IVP).

God's wrath and judgement are not the final word. He will not destroy his people lest the heathen rejoice and despise the Lord (26,27). And when God has finished using the heathen nations as his instrument of judgement on Israel, then he will turn with compassion and vindicate his people.

TO THINK OVER: Are there ways in which we treat religion as an optional extra?

33 The blessing of the tribes

The chapter begins and ends with words of praise to the Lord whose fiery power (2) and gentle love (3) are typified by the fact that he is 'king' and that he calls Israel 'Jeshurun' (5,26; 32:15), an affectionate name meaning 'upright'. His majesty is unique (26) and he protects his people from their enemies (27). Christians also may rejoice that 'underneath are the everlasting arms', for we, too, are a 'people saved by the Lord, the shield of your help' (29).

Moses' final act of solemn benediction has a patriarchal air, reminding us of Genesis 48 and 49. Such a blessing was not mere words; the words were charged with power which would certainly be fulfilled. As with God's word, so with patriarchal blessings – the word does not return empty (Isa. 55:11).

There is a problem with regard to the dating of this chapter. It contains several ancient linguistic features, but some of its contents point to a later compilation – for example, the placing of the tribe of Dan in the north (compare Judg. 18). Perhaps the answer is that the basic contents are the words of Moses, but a later editor has developed them in the light of ensuing historical happenings.

While Simeon is inexplicably missing from the blessing, Joseph, with his sons Ephraim and Manasseh, is specially blessed in his abundantly fertile inheritance in the hills (13-17). Hosea 12:8 demonstrates the reality of the wealth here prophesied, but also illustrates how easily riches and guilt can be interlocked.

As we might expect, the brief blessing of Benjamin (12) is particularly loving, showing the close relationship this tribe had with the Lord himself. It was not only true that Benjamin dwelt in the Lord, but also Yahweh made his dwelling inside the borders of Benjamin, for the Temple lay just within their territory.

The final benediction falls upon Asher with the wish that he may be blessed above his brethren. Honour and favour are linked to prosperity from an abundance of oil (24). The Galilean highlands which they inhabited were renowned for their olives. But Asher would not become soft in her favoured position, for she was to be characterised also by 'iron and bronze' (25) with fully sufficient strength for the needs of each day. The Christian likewise can trust the Lord that 'as your days, so shall your strength be'.

34 The death of Moses

Although it is clear that this chapter was written by someone other than Moses (note again the reference to Moses in the third person) and apparently a considerable time after Moses' death (10), yet the greater part of Deuteronomy consists of the carefully preserved words of Moses himself (31:24-26).

Moses' life of 120 years divides neatly into three periods – forty years was reckoned to be the span of a generation. The preparatory period of the first eighty years included the wealth and education of Egypt as well as relative poverty and solitude while keeping Jethro's flocks. The character formation of those early years made possible the wise leadership of an undisciplined people through the wilderness wanderings. The frustration of long years of preparation is often a necessary prelude to a life of service.

The closing description of Moses is impressive (10-12). Although he was noted for his supreme meekness (Num. 12:3) he was also a man of 'mighty power' whose deeds were 'great and terrible' (12). Meek humility need not necessarily be equated with softness. We have already noted how Moses' words often foresaw and predicted future developments, so we are not surprised to read that he was 'a prophet' (10). The source of his greatness lay in his intimate personal relationship with the Lord, which is so beautifully described – 'whom the Lord knew face to face'.

This chapter does not merely look backwards in memory of the great Moses; it also looks forward as Moses' commissioning of Joshua (9) inaugurates a new era in the history of Israel. Joshua not only had the position of leadership, but also the charisma needed for his ministry – he was 'full of the spirit of wisdom'. Position alone is inadequate to ensure a right obedience from the people, but the added gift of the fullness of the spirit of wisdom leads to 'so the people of Israel obeyed him' (9).

THOUGHT: The frustration of long years of preparation is often a necessary prelude to a life of service.

Questions for further study and discussion on Deuteronomy 27–34

1. Think through Old Testament history and see how many of the threats in chapter 28 were literally fulfilled. How far do they relate to our society today?

2. When the 'root of bitterness' begins to grow in us or others what can we do about it (Heb. 12:15, and note on Deut. 29)?

3. 'The centrality of the written word of God is vital for the spiritual health of God's people' (note on Deut. 31). Why is this so? Discuss the methods of Bible Study you find most helpful.

4. What is the relationship between demons, idols and the deities of non-Christian religions (compare ch. 32)?

5. Think through the significance for Israel of, 'it is no trifle for you, but it is your life' (32:47) and apply this to your own circumstances.

6. How can we know that the promises of Deuteronomy 33 apply to us (compare John 6:37)?

7. Contrast Moses' vision of 'all the land' (34:1) with Matthew 4:8.

8. What have you found most challenging and most encouraging in your study of Deuteronomy?